Modern Critical Views

Modern Critical Views

ITALO CALVINO

Edited and with an introduction by
Harold Bloom
Sterling Professor of the Humanities
Yale University

CHELSEA HOUSE PUBLISHERS
Philadelphia

© 2001 by Chelsea House Publishers, a subsidiary of
Haights Cross Communications.

Introduction © 2001 by Harold Bloom.

Printed and bound in the United States of America

10 9 8 7 6 5 4 3 2 1

∞ The paper used in this publication meets the minimum
requirements of the American National Standard for
Permanence of Paper for Printed Library Materials,
Z39.48-1984

Library of Congress Cataloging-in-Publication Data

Italo Calvino / Harold Bloom, editor.
       p. cm. — (Modern Critical Views)
     Collection of previously published essays.
     Includes bibliographical references and index.
     ISBN 0-7910-5919-7
     1. Calvino, Italo—Criticism and interpretation.
  I. Bloom, Harold.   II. Series.

  PQ4809.A45 Z749 2000
  853'.914—dc21   00-031422
                                              CIP

Chelsea House Publishers
1974 Sproul Road, Suite 400
Broomall, PA 19008-0914

The Chelsea House World Wide Web address is
http://www.chelseahouse.com

Contributing editors: Hillary Kelleher, Tenley Williams

Produced by: Robert Gerson Publisher's Services, Santa Barbara, CA

Contents

Editor's Note

This volume gathers together a representative selection of the best criticism available in English upon the writing of Italo Calvino. The critical essays are reprinted here in the chronological order of their original publication. I am grateful to Hillary Kelleher and Tenley Williams for their aid in my editing of this book.

My Introduction centers upon the novel *Invisible Cities* and the short story "The Night Driver" in *t zero*, finding in them the antipodes of Calvino's vision of "who and what, in the midst of the inferno, are not inferno." The chronological sequence of criticism begins with an overview by the novelist Gore Vidal, who praises Calvino as a true mediator between fantasy and everyday life.

Angela M. Jeannet and Teresa de Lauretis both concentrate upon *Invisible Cities*, with its simultaneous reliance upon, and mockery of, semiotic models. For Olga Ragusa, Calvino resembles Pirandello in his preference for images rather than ideas. Linda C. Badley explores the intricate trap that reading constitutes in *If On a Winter's Night a Traveler*.

The distinguished Irish poet Seamus Heaney, reviewing *Mr. Palomar*, finds much to admire in the book's audacity, after which *Cosmicomics*, Calvino's narration upon science fiction, is studied by John Dolis. This volume concludes with Michael Wood's agile depiction of the relation in Calvino between criticism and fiction.

Introduction

The era of our contemporary modes of literary criticism will pass; perhaps already it has passed. Fictions that accommodate themselves too readily in regard to our modes will pass with them. Nabokov, Borges, García Márquez, John Barth may seem less available to generations later than our own. Much of Italo Calvino doubtless will dwindle away also, but not *Invisible Cities*, though aspects of the book might almost be judged as having been written for sensibilities schooled by semiotics and by reader-response criticism. But those aspects are not central to *Invisible Cities*, and this work's outer armature will not engage me here. Like much of Kafka, *Invisible Cities* will survive its admirers' modes of apprehension, because it returns us to the pure form of romance, genre of the marvelous, realm of speculation. With Kafka's *The Great Wall of China*, it renews a literature we require yet can no longer deserve or earn.

Like Kublai Khan, we do not necessarily believe everything that Marco Polo describes, but we too suffer the emptiness of the evening land and hope to discern the tracery of some pattern that will compensate us for our endless errors about life. Doubtless, as Nietzsche remarked, errors about life are necessary for life, and doubtless also, as Emerson said, we demand victory, a victory to the senses as well as to the soul. But error and triumph alike induce emptiness, the cosmological emptiness that Gnosticism named as the *kenoma*, the waste land or waste wilderness of all literary romance. Calvino's Kublai Khan is a Demiurge inhabiting that *kenoma*, "an endless formless ruin," in which we know that "corruption's gangrene has spread too far to be healed by our scepter, that the triumph over enemy sovereigns has made us the heirs of their long undoing."

The Invisible Cities dot the *kenoma*, but are no part of it, being sparks of the original Abyss, our foremother and forefather, and so the source of everything still that is best and oldest in us. It is not in the *kenoma* that "the foreigner hesitating between two women always encounters a third" or where you find "bergamot, sturgeon roe, astrolabes, amethysts." As sparks of

1

the true *pneuma* or breath-soul, the Invisible Cities are not psyches or personalities, despite their names. They do not represent women but rather forewomen, as it were, for in truth all of them are at once memories, desires, and signs, that is, repressions and the return of the repressed. Perhaps it is Calvino's peculiar genius (though he shares it with Kafka) that we scarcely can distinguish, in his pages, the repressed and its return, as here in the city called Anastasia:

> At the end of three days, moving southward, you come upon Anastasia, a city with concentric canals watering it and kites flying over it. I should now list the wares that can profitably be bought here: agate, onyx, chrysoprase, and other varieties of chalcedony; I should praise the flesh of the golden pheasant cooked here over fires of seasoned cherry wood and sprinkled with much sweet marjoram; and tell of the women I have seen bathing in the pool of a garden and who sometimes—it is said— invite the stranger to disrobe with them and chase them in the water. But with all this, I would not be telling you the city's true essence; for while the description of Anastasia awakens desires one at a time only to force you to stifle them, when you are in the heart of Anastasia one morning your desires waken all at once and surround you. The city appears to you as a whole where no desire is lost and of which you are a part, and since it enjoys everything you do not enjoy, you can do nothing but inhabit this desire and be content. Such is the power, sometimes called malignant, sometimes benign, that Anastasia, the treacherous city, possesses; if for eight hours a day you work as a cutter of agate, onyx, chrysoprase, your labor which gives form to desire takes from desire its form, and you believe you are enjoying Anastasia wholly when you are only its slave.

That antithetical will, seen by Nietzsche as art's willed revenge against time, triumphs here even as it does in Yeats or Kafka. The Great Khan, Kublai, learns from Marco that his empire is nothing but a summa of emblems, a zodiac of phantasmagorias. Learning all the emblems will give Kublai no sense of possession, for on the day of total knowledge, the Khan will be an emblem among emblems, at once again the sign of repression and of return from such defense. Marco's use, both for himself and for Kublai, is to teach what he uniquely learns: that the meaning of any Invisible City can only be another Invisible City, not itself:

And Marco's answer was: "Elsewhere is a negative mirror. The traveler recognizes the little bit that is his, discovering the much he has not had and will never have."

As Marco's narration proceeds, the Invisible Cities accomplish the paradox of growing ever more fantastic, yet ever more pragmatic. Calvino remembers implicitly Nietzsche's dark aphorism: we only find words to describe what we now feel contempt towards, however dearly we once held it in our hearts. The Khan reminds Marco that he never mentions Venice, and the traveler reveals the secret of every quester for the Alien God, for the City forever lost:

"Memory's images, once they are fixed in words, are erased," Polo said. "Perhaps I am afraid of losing Venice all at once, if I speak of it. Or perhaps, speaking of other cities, I have already lost it, little by little."

It is fitting that Calvino's last Invisible City should be his most imaginative, or perhaps it is merely that he has described my own dream, the extraordinary Berenice, at once the unjust city, and the city of the just. Berenice is a nightmare of repetitions, in which the just and the unjust constantly undergo metamorphoses into one another:

From these data it is possible to deduce an image of the future Berenice, which will bring you closer to knowing the truth than any other information about the city as it is seen today. You must nevertheless bear in mind what I am about to say to you: in the seed of the city of the just, a malignant seed is hidden, in its turn: the certainty and pride of being in the right—and of being more just than many others who call themselves more just than the just. This seed ferments in bitterness, rivalry, resentment; and the natural desire of revenge on the unjust is colored by a yearning to be in their place and to act as they do. Another unjust city, though different from the first, is digging out its space within the double sheath of the unjust and just Berenices.
    Having said this, I do not wish your eyes to catch a distorted image, so I must draw your attention to an intrinsic quality of this unjust city germinating secretly inside the secret just city: and this is the possible awakening—as if in an excited opening of windows—of a later love for justice, not yet subjected to rules,

capable of reassembling a city still more just than it was before it
became the vessel of injustice. But if you peer deeper into this new
germ of justice you can discern a tiny spot that is spreading like the
mounting tendency to impose what is just through what is unjust,
and perhaps this is the germ of an immense metropolis. . . .

From my words you will have reached the conclusion that
the real Berenice is a temporal succession of different cities,
alternately just and unjust. But what I wanted to warn you about
is something else: all the future Berenices are already present in
this instant, wrapped one within the other, confined, crammed,
inextricable.

This is not merely a parable about the relativity of justice, or the selfish
virtue of self-righteousness, but a vision of the ambivalence of all Eros, since
the just Berenice is an Eros, and the unjust a Thanatos. Just and unjust,
Berenice is the city of jealousy, of natural possessiveness, of the malignant
seed hidden in the heart of Eros. The shadow of our mortality, cast upwards
by the earth into the heavens, stopped at the sphere of Venus, as Shelley liked
to remind us, but in Berenice the shadow never stops. A temporal succession
of love and death, just and unjust, is real enough, and dark enough. But
Calvino gives us a stronger warning: every instant holds all the future
Berenices, inextricably crammed together, death drive and libido confined in
one chiasmus, wrapped one within the other. Fortunately, *Invisible Cities* ends
more amiably, when Marco insists that the inferno need not be the last
landing place, if only we: "seek and learn to recognize who and what, in the
midst of the inferno, are not inferno, then make them endure, give them
space." Dante would have dismissed this with grim irony, but we cannot
afford to do so.

As coda, I resort to an extraordinary short story, "The Night Driver,"
in Calvino's *t zero*. The narrator, in a telephone argument with Y, his
mistress, tells her he wishes to end their affair. Y replies that she will phone
Z, the narrator's rival. To save the affair, the narrator undertakes a night drive
on the superhighway that connects his city to that of his beloved. In rain and
darkness, at high speed, the narrator does not know if Z is outspeeding him
towards Y, or if Y herself perhaps started towards his city, with motives akin
to his own. In a mad parody of semiotics, the narrator, Y, and Z have become
signs or signals or messages, weird reductions in a system:

Naturally, if I were absolutely alone on this superhighway, if I
saw no other cars speeding in either direction, then everything
would be much clearer, I would be certain that Z hasn't moved

to supplant me, nor has Y moved to make peace with me, facts I might register as positive or negative in my accounting, but which would in any case leave no room for doubt. And yet if I had the power of exchanging my present state of uncertainty for such a negative certainty, I would refuse the bargain without hesitation. The ideal condition for excluding every doubt would prevail if in this part of the world there existed only three automobiles: mine, Y's, and Z's; then no other car could proceed in my direction except Z's, and the only car heading in the opposite direction would surely be Y's. Instead, among the hundreds of cars that the night and the rain reduce to anonymous glimmers, only a motionless observer situated in a favorable position could distinguish one car from the other and perhaps recognize who is inside. This is the contradiction in which I find myself: if I want to receive a message I must give up being a message myself, but the message I want to receive from Y—namely, that Y has made herself into a message—has value only if I in turn am a message, and on the other hand the message I am has meaning only if Y doesn't limit herself to receiving it like any ordinary receiver of messages but if she also is that message I am waiting to receive from her.

By now to arrive in B, go up to Y's house, find that she has remained there with her headache brooding over the causes of our quarrel, would give me no satisfaction; if then Z were to arrive also a scene would be the result, histrionic and loathsome; and if instead I were to find out that Z has prudently stayed home or that Y didn't carry out her threat to telephone him, I would feel I had played the fool. On the other hand, if I had remained in A, and Y had gone there to apologize to me, I would have seen Y through different eyes, a weak woman, clinging to me, and something between us would have changed. I can no longer accept any situation other than this transformation of ourselves into the messages of ourselves. And what about Z? Even Z must not escape our fate, he too must be transformed into the message of himself; it would be terrible if I were to run to Y jealous of Z and if Y were running to me, repentant, avoiding Z, while actually Z hasn't remotely thought of stirring from his house.

To be made into a message, or to give up such a making, alike are catastrophe creations. Calvino's sublimely funny summary seems to me his finest sentence ever: "I can no longer accept any situation other than the transformation of ourselves into the messages of ourselves." But are we not then back in the City of Berenice? Y, Z, and the narrator are all residents of that Invisible City, where the just and the unjust twine into one another, love cannot be distinguished from jealousy, and repression scarcely can be told from what returns from it. Night drivers go between Invisible Cities, transforming memory and desire into homogenous signs, confounding eyes and names, contaminating the sky with the dead. The alternative to such night driving indeed is to "seek and learn to recognize who and what, in the midst of the inferno, are not inferno, then make them endure, give them space."

GORE VIDAL

Fabulous Calvino

Calvino's first novel, ⟨*The Path to the Nest of Spiders*,⟩ is a plainly told, exuberant sort of book. Although the writing is conventional, there is an odd intensity in the way Calvino sees things, a closeness of scrutiny much like that of William Golding. Like Golding he knows how and when to *inhabit* entirely, with all senses functioning, landscape, state of mind, act. In *The Spire* Golding makes the flawed church so real that one smells the mortar, sees the motes of dust, fears for the ill-placed stones. Calvino does the same in his story of Pin, a boy living on the Ligurian coast of Italy, near San Remo (although Calvino was brought up in San Remo, he was actually born in Cuba, a detail given by none of his American publishers; no doubt in deference to our attempted conquest of that unfortunate island).

Pin lives with his sister, a prostitute. He spends his days at a low-life bar where he amuses with songs and taunts the grownups, a race of monsters as far as he is concerened, but he has no other companions for "Pin is a boy who does not know how to play games, and cannot take part in the games either of children or grownups." Pin dreams, however, of "a friend, a real friend who understands him and whom he can understand, and then to him, and only to him, will he show the place where the spiders have their lairs."

From *The New York Review of Books* 21, no. 9 (30 May 1974). © 1974 by *The New York Review of Books*.

It's on a stony little path which winds down to the torrent
between earthy grassy slopes. There, in the grass, the spiders
make their nests in tunnels lined with dry grass. But the
wonderful thing is that the nests have tiny doors, also made of
dried grass, tiny round doors which can open and shut.

This sort of precise, quasi-scientific observation keeps Calvino from the sort
of sentimentality that was prevalent in the Forties, when wise children
learned compassion from a black mammy as she deep-fried chitlins and Jesus
in equal parts south of the Mason-Dixon line.

Pin joins the partisans in the hills above the Ligurian coast. I have a
suspicion that Calvino is dreaming all this for he writes like a bookish, nearsighted man who has mislaid his glasses: objects held close to are vividly
described but the middle and far distances of landscape and war tend to blur.
It makes no difference, however, for the dreams of a nearsighted young man
at the beginning of a literary career can be more real to the reader than the
busy reportage of those journalist-novelists who were there and, seeing it all,
saw nothing.

Although Calvino manages to inhabit the skin of the outraged and
outrageous child, his men and women are almost always shadowy. Later in
his career, Calvino will eliminate men and women altogether as he re-creates
the cosmos. Meanwhile, as a beginner, he is a vivid, if occasionally clumsy,
writer. Two thirds of the way through the narrative he shifts the point of view
from Pin to a pair of commissars who would have been more effective had he
observed them from outside. Then, confusingly, he shifts again, briefly, into
the mind of a traitor who is about to be shot. Finally, he returns us to Pin just
as the boy finds the longed-for friend, a young partisan called Cousin who
takes him in hand not only literally but, presumably, for the rest of the time
Pin will need to grow up. Calvino's last paragraphs are almost always jubi-
lant—the sort of cheerful codas that only a deep pessimist about human
matters could write. But then Calvino, like one of Pin's friends, Red Wolf,
"belongs to the generation brought up on strip cartoons; he has taken them
all seriously and life has not disproved them so far."

In 1952 Calvino published *The Cloven Viscount*, one of the three short novels
he has since collected under the title *Our Ancestors*. They are engaging works,
written in a style somewhat like that of T. H. White's Arthurian novels. The
narrator of *The Cloven Viscount* is, again, an orphan boy. During a war
between Austria and Turkey (1716) the boy's uncle Viscount Medardo was
cloven from top to crotch by a cannon ball. Saved by doctors on the battle-
field, the half Viscount was sent home with one leg, one arm, one eye, half a

nose, mouth, etc. En route, Calvino pays homage (ironic?) to Malaparte ("The patch of plain they were crossing was covered with horses' carcasses, some supine with hooves to the sky, others prone with muzzles dug into the earth." A nice reprise of those dead horses in *The Skin*).

The story is cheerfully, briskly told. The Half Viscount is a perfect bastard and takes pleasure in murder, fire, torture. He burns down part of his own castle, hoping to incinerate his old nurse Sebastiana; finally, he packs her off to a leper colony. He tries to poison his nephew. He never stops slashing living creatures in half. He has a thing about halfness.

> If only I could halve every whole thing like this," said my uncle, lying face down on the rocks, stroking the convulsive half of an octopus, "so that everyone could escape from his obtuse and ignorant wholeness. I was whole and all things were natural and confused to me, stupid as the air; I thought I was seeing all and it was only the outside rind. If you ever become a half of yourself, and I hope you do for your own sake, my boy, you'll understand things beyond the common intelligence of brains that are whole. You'll have lost half of yourself and of the world, but the remaining half will be a thousand times deeper and more precious."

I note that the publisher's blurb would have us believe that this is "an allegory of modern man—alienated and mutilated—this novel has profound overtones. As a parody of the Christian parables of good and evil, it is both witty and refreshing." Well, at least the book is witty and refreshing. Actually the story is less Christian than a send-up of Plato and his idea of the whole.

In due course the other half of the Viscount hits town; this half is unbearably good and deeply boring. He, too, is given to celebrating halfness because, "One understands the sorrow of every person and thing in the world at its own incompleteness. I was whole and did not understand. . . ." A charming young girl named Pamela (homage to Richardson) is beloved by both halves of the Viscount; but she has serious reservations about each. "Doing good together is the only way to love," intones the good half. To which the irritable girl responds, "A pity. I thought there were other ways." When the two halves are finally united, the resulting whole Viscount is the usual not very interesting human mixture. In a happy ending, he marries Pamela. But the boy narrator is not content. "Amid all this fervor of wholeness, [I] felt myself growing sadder and more lacking. Sometimes one who thinks himself incomplete is merely young."

The Cloven Viscount is filled with many closely observed natural images like "The subsoil was so full of ants that a hand put down anywhere came up all black and swarming with them." I don't know which was written first, *The Cloven Viscount* (1952) or "The Argentine Ant," published in *Botteghe Oscure* (1952), but Calvino's nightmare of an ant-infested world touched on in the novel becomes the subject of "The Argentine Ant" and I fear that I must now trot out that so often misused word "masterpiece." Or, put another way, if "The Argentine Ant" is not a masterpiece of twentieth-century prose writing, I cannot think of anything better. Certainly it is as minatory and strange as anything by Kafka. It is also hideously funny. In some forty pages Calvino gives us "the human condition," as the blurb writers would say, in spades. That is, the human condition *today*. Or the dilemma of modern man. Or the disrupted environment. Or nature's revenge. Or an allegory of grace. Whatever. . . . But a story is, finally, what it tells and no more.

Calvino's first sentence is rather better than God's "in the beginning was the word." God (as told to Saint John) has always had a penchant for cloudy abstractions of the sort favored by American novelists, heavyweight division—unlike Calvino who simply tells us what's what: "When we came to settle here we did not know about the ants." No nonsense about here or we. *Here* is a place infested with ants and *we* are the nuclear family: father, mother, child. No names.

"We" have rented a house in a town where our Uncle Augusto used to hang out. Uncle Augusto rather liked the place, though he did say, "You should see the ants over there . . . they're not like the ones here, those ants. . . ." But we paid no attention at the time. As the local landlady Signora Mauro shows the young couple about the house they have just rented from her she distracts their attention from the walls with a long dissertation on the gas meter. When she has gone, the baby is put to bed and the young couple take a stroll outside. Their next-door neighbor is spraying the plants in his garden with a bellows. The ants, he explains, "as if not wanting to make it sound important."

The young couple return to their house and find it infested with ants. The Argentine ants. The husband-narrator suddenly recalls that this country is known for them. "It comes from South America," he adds, helpfully, to his distraught wife. Finally, they go to bed without "the feeling we were starting a new life, only a sense of dragging on into a future full of new troubles."

The rest of the story deals with the way that the others in the valley cope with the ants. Some go in for poisons; others make fantastic contraptions to confuse or kill the insects while for twenty years the Argentine Ant Control Corporation's representative has been putting out molasses ostensibly to control (kill) the ants but many believe that this is done to *feed* the

ants. The frantic young couple pay a call on Signora Mauro in her dim pala-
tial drawing room. She is firm; ants do not exist in well-tended houses, but
from the way she squirms in her chair it is plain that the ants are crawling
about under her clothes.

Methodically, Calvino describes the various human responses to The
Condition. There is the Christian Scientist ignoring of all evidence; the
Manichean acceptance of evil; the relentless Darwinian faith that genetic
superiority will prevail. But the ants prove indestructible and the story ends
with the family going down to the seaside where there are no ants; where

> The water was calm; with just a slight continual change of color,
> blue and black, darker farthest away. I thought of the expanses of
> water like this, of the infinite grains of soft sand down there at
> the bottom of the sea where the currents leave white shells
> washed clean by the waves.

I don't know what this coda means. I also see no reason for it to mean. A
contrast has been made between the ant-infested valley and the cool serenity
of mineral and of shell beneath the sea, that other air we can no longer
breathe since our ancestors chose to live upon the land.

In 1956 Calvino edited a volume of Italian fables, and the local critics
decided that he was true heir to Grimm. Certainly the bright, deadly fairy
tale attracts him and he returned to it with *The Baron in the Trees* (1957). Like
the other two tales in the trilogy, the story is related in the first person: this
time by the eponymous baron's brother. The time is 1767. The place Liguria.
The Baron is Cosimo Piovasco di Rondò, who after an argument at dinner
on June 15 decides to live in the trees. The response of family and friends to
this decision is varied. But Cosimo is content. Later he goes in for politics;
deals with Napoleon himself: becomes legend.

Calvino has now developed two ways of writing. One is literally fabulous.
The other makes use of a dry rather didactic style in which the detail is as
precisely observed as if the author were writing a manual for the construction of a solar heating unit. Yet the premises of the "dry" stories are often
quite as fantastic as those of the fairy tales.

"Smog" was published in 1958, a long time before the current preoc-
cupation with man's systematic destruction of the environment. The narrator
comes to a large city to take over a small magazine called *Purification*. The
owner of the magazine, Commendatore Cordà, is an important manufac-
turer who produces the sort of air pollution that his magazine would like to
eliminate. Cordà has it both ways and his new editor settles in nicely. The

prevailing image of the story is smog: gray dust covers everything; nothing is ever clean. The city is very like the valley of the Argentine ants but on a larger scale for now a vast population is slowly strangling in the fumes of its industry, of the combustion engine.

Calvino is finely comic as he shows us the publisher instructing his editor in how to strike the right tone. "We are not utopians, mind you, we are practical men." Or, "It's a battle for an ideal." Or, "There will not be (nor has there ever been) any contradiction between an economy in free, natural expansion and the hygiene necessary to the human organism . . . between the smoke of our productive factories and the green of our incomparable natural beauty. . . ." Finally, the editorial policy is set. "We are one of the cities where the problem of air pollution is most serious, but at the same time we are the city where most is being done to counteract the situation. At the same time you understand!" By some fifteen years, Calvino anticipated Exxon's double-talk ads on American television

This is the first of Calvino's stories where a realistic affair takes place between a man and a woman—well, fairly realistic. We never know how the elegant and wealthy Claudia came to meet the narrator or what she sees in him; yet, periodically, she descends upon him, confuses him ("to embrace her, I had removed my glasses"). One day they drive out of the city. The narrator comments on the ugliness of the city and the ubiquitous smog. Claudia says the "people have lost the sense of beauty." He answers, "Beauty has to be constantly invented." They argue; he finds everything cruel. Later, he meets a proletarian who is in arms against Cordà. The narrator admires the worker Omar, admires "the stubborn ones, the tough ones." But Calvino does not really *engage*, in Sartre's sense. He suspects that the trap we are in is too great for mere politics to spring.

The narrator begins to write about atomic radiation in the atmosphere; about the way the weather is changing in the world. Is there a connection? Even Cordà is momentarily alarmed. But then life goes on, for is not Cordà himself "the smog's master? It was he who blew it out constantly over the city," and his magazine was "born of the need to give those working to produce the smog some hope of a life that was not all smog, and yet, at the same time, to celebrate its power."

The story's coda resembles that of "The Argentine Ant." The narrator goes to the outskirts of the city where the women are doing laundry. The sight is cheering. "It wasn't much, but for me, seeking only images to retain in my eyes, perhaps it was enough."

The next year Calvino switched to his other manner. *The Nonexistent Knight* is the last of the *Our Ancestors* trilogy though it comes first chronologically, in the age of Charlemagne. Again a war is going on. We are not introduced to the narrator until page 34—Sister Theodora is a nun in a convent who has been assigned to tell this story "for the health of the soul." Unfortunately, the plot is giving her a good deal of trouble because "we nuns have few occasions to speak with soldiers. . . . Apart from religious ceremonies, triduums, novenas, gardening, harvesting, vintaging, whippings, slavery, incest, fires, hangings, invasions, sacking, rape and pestilence, we have had no experience."

Sister Theodora does her best with the tale of Agiluf, a knight who does not exist. What does exist is a suit of white armor from which comes the voice of Agiluf. He is a devoted knight in the service of Charlemagne who thinks him a bit much but graciously concedes, "for someone who doesn't exist, you seem in fine form." Since Agiluf has no appetites or weaknesses, he is the perfect soldier and so disliked by all. As for Agiluf, "people's bodies gave him a disagreeable feeling resembling envy, but also a stab of pride of contemptuous superiority." A young man (an older version of Pin, of the cloven Viscount's nephew) named Raimbaut joins the army to avenge his father's death. Agiluf gives him dull advice. There are battles. General observations. "What is war, after all, but this passing of more and more dented objects from hand to hand?" Then a meeting with a man who confuses himself with things outside himself. When he drinks soup, he becomes soup; thinks he is soup to be drunk in turn: "the world being nothing but a vast shapeless mass of soup in which all things dissolved."

Calvino now strikes a theme which will be developed in later works. The confusion between "I"/"it"; "I"/"you"; the arbitrariness of naming things, of categorizing, and of setting apart, particularly when "World conditions were still confused in the era when this book took place. It was not rare then to find names and thoughts and forms and institutions that corresponded to nothing in existence. But at the same time the world was polluted with objects and capacities and persons who lacked any name or distinguishing mark."

A triangle occurs. Raimbaut falls in love with a knight who proves to be a young woman, Bradamante. Unfortunately, *she* falls in love with Agiluf, the nonexistent knight. At this point there is rather too much plot for Sister Theodora, who strikes the professional writer's saddest note. "One starts off writing with a certain zest, but a time comes when the pen merely grates in dusty ink, and not a drop of life flows, and life is all outside, outside the window, outside oneself, and it seems that never more can one escape into a page one is writing, open out another world, leap the gap."

But the teller finally gets a grip on the tale; closes the gap. Knightly quests are conducted, concluded. Agiluf surrenders his armor and ceases to be; Raimbaut is allowed to inhabit the armor. Bradamante has vanished, but with a fine *coup de théâtre* Sister Theodora reveals to us that *she* is Bradamante, who is now rushing the narrative to its end so that she can take the beloved white armor in her arms: aware that it now contains the young and passionate Raimbaut, her true love. "That is why my pen at a certain point began running on so. I rush to meet him. . . . A page is good only when we turn it and find life urging along. . . ."

With the completion of the trilogy, Calvino took to his other manner and wrote "The Watcher," the most realistic of his stories and the most overtly political. The narrator has a name, Amerigo Ormea. He is a poll watcher in Turin for the Communist party during the national election of 1953. Amerigo's poll is inside the vast "Cottolengo Hospital for Incurables." Apparently the mad and the senile and even the comatose are allowed to vote ("hospitals, asylums and convents had served as great reservoirs of votes for the Christian Democrat party"). Amerigo is a serene observer of democracy's confusions, having "learned that change, in politics, comes through long and complex processes"; he also confesses that "acquiring experience had meant becoming slightly pessimistic."

In the course of the day, Amerigo observes with fine dispassion the priests and nuns as they herd their charges into the polling booths that have been set up inside the hospital. Despite the grotesqueries of the situation, Amerigo takes some pleasure in the matter-of-factness of the voting, for "in Italy, which had always bowed and scraped before every form of pomp, display, sumptuousness, ornament, this seemed to him finally the lesson of an honest, austere morality, and a perpetual, silent revenge on the Fascists. . . ; now they had fallen into dust with all their gold fringe and their ribbons, while democracy, with its stark ceremony of pieces of paper folded over like telegrams, of pencils given to callused or shaky hands, went ahead."

But for the watcher boredom eventually sets in: it is a long day. "Amerigo felt a yearning need for beauty, which became focused in the thought of his mistress Lia." He contemplates Lia in reverie. "What is this need of ours for beauty? Amerigo asked himself." Apparently Calvino has not advanced much beyond the last dialogue in "Smog." He contemplates the perfection of classical Greece but recalls that the Greeks destroyed deformed children, redundant girls. Obviously placing beauty too high in the scale of values is "a step toward an inhuman civilization, which will then sentence the deformed to be thrown off a cliff."

When another poll watcher remarks to Amerigo that the mad all must recognize one another in Cottolengo, he slips into reverie: "They would remember that humanity could be a different thing, as in fables, a world of giants, an Olympus. . . . As we do: and perhaps, without realizing it, we are deformed, backward, compared to a different, forgotten form of existence. . . ." What is human, what is real?

Calvino's vision is usually presented in fantastic terms but now he becomes unusually concrete. Since he has elected to illuminate an actual time and place (Italy between 1945 and the election of 1953) he is able to spell it out. "In those years the Italian Communist party, among its many other tasks, had also assumed the position of an ideal liberal party, which had never really existed. And so the bosom of each individual communist could house two personalities at once: an intrasigent revolutionary and an Olympian liberal." Amerigo's pessimism derives from the obvious fact that the two do not go together. I am reminded of Alexander Herzen's comment about the Latins: they do not want liberty, they want to sue for liberty.

Amerigo goes home to lunch (he has a maid who cooks and serves! Written in 1963 about the events of 1953, this is plainly a historical novel). He looks for a book to read. "Pure literature" is out. "Personal literature now seemed to him a row of tombstones in a cemetery: the literature of the living as well as of the dead. Now he sought something else from books: the wisdom of the ages or simply something that helped to understand something." He takes a stab at Marx's *Youthful Writings*. "Man's universality appears, practically speaking, in that same universe that makes all nature man's *inorganic* body. . . . Nature is man's *inorganic body* precisely because it is not his human body." Thus genius turns everything into itself. As Marx invented Kapital from capitalism, so Calvino turns a passage of Marx into Calvino himself: the man who drinks soup is the soup that drinks him. Wholeness is all.

Fortified with this reassuring text, Amerigo endures a telephone conversation with Lia. It is the usual quibbling conversation between Calvino protagonist and Calvino mistress. She tells him that she is pregnant. "Amerigo was an ardent supporter of birth control, even though his party's attitude on the subject was either agnostic or hostile. Nothing shocked him so much as the ease with which people multiply, and the more hungry and backward, the more they keep having children. . . ." In the land of Margaret Sanger this point of view is not exactly startling, but for an Italian communist a dozen years ago, the sense of a world dying of too many children, of too much "smog" was a monstrous revelation. At this point, Amerigo rounds on both the Bible and Marx as demented celebrators of human fecundity.

Amerigo returns to the hospital; observes children shaped like fish and again wonders at what point is a human being human. Finally the day ends; the voting is done. Amerigo looks out over the complex of hospital buildings and notes that the reddish sun appeared to open "perspectives of a city that had never been seen." Thus the Calvino coda strikes its first familiar chord. Laughing women cross the courtyard with a caldron, "perhaps the evening soup. Even the ultimate city of imperfection has its perfect hour, the watcher thought, the hour, the moment, when every city is the City."

Most realistic and specific of Calvino's works, "The Watcher" has proved (to date) to be the last of the "dry" narratives. In 1965 Calvino published *Cosmicomics:* twelve brief stories dealing in a fantastic way with the creation of the universe, man, society. Like Pin's young friend who decided that life indeed resembles the strip cartoon, Calvino has deployed his complex prose in order to compose in words a super strip cartoon narrated by Qfvfq whose progress from life inside the first atom to mollusk on the earth's sea floor to social-climbing amphibian to dinosaur to moon-farmer is told in a dozen episodes that are entirely unlike anything that anyone else has written since, perhaps, Lucian.

"At Daybreak" is the story of the creation of the universe as viewed by Qfvfq and his mysterious tribe consisting of a father, mother, sister, brother, Granny, as well as acquaintances—formless sentiencies who inhabit the universal dust that is on the verge of becoming the nebula which will contain our solar system. Where and who *they* are is, literally, obscure since light has not yet been invented. So "there was nothing to do but wait, keep covered as best we could, doze, speak out now and then to make sure we were all still there; and, naturally, scratch ourselves; because—they can say what they like—all those particles spinning around had only one effect, a troublesome itching." That itch starts to change things. Condensation begins. Also, confusion: Granny loses her cushion, "a little ellipsoid of galactic matter." Things clot; nickel is formed; members of the tribe start flying off in all directions. Suddenly the condensation is complete and light breaks. The sun is now in its place and the planets begin their orbits "and, above all, it was deathly hot."

As the earth starts to gell, Qfvfq's sister takes fright and vanishes inside the planet and is not heard from again "until I met her, much later, at Canberra in 1912, married to a certain Sullivan, a retired railroad man, so changed I hardly recognized her."

The early Calvino was much like his peers Pavese and Vittorini—writers who tended to reflect the realistic storytelling of Hemingway and Dos Passos. Then Calvino moved to Paris where he found his own voice or voices and became, to a degree, infected by the French. Since the writing of *Our Ancestors* and the three stories that make up *The Watcher*, Calvino has been influenced, variously, by Barthes and the semeiologists, by Borges, and by the now old New Novel. In *Cosmicomics* these influences are generally benign since Calvino is too formidable and original an artist to be derailed by theoreticians or undone by the example of another creator. Nevertheless the story "A Sign in Space" comes perilously close to being altogether too reverent an obeisance to semeiology.

As the sun takes two hundred million years to revolve around the galaxy, Qfvfq becomes obsessed with making a sign in space, something peculiarly his own to mark his passage as well as something that would impress anyone who might be watching. His ambition is the result of a desire to think because "to think something had never been possible, first because there were no things to think about, and second because signs to think of them by were lacking, but from the moment there was that sign, it was possible for someone thinking to think of a sign, and therefore that one, in the sense that the sign was the thing you could think about and also the sign of the thing thought, namely, itself." So he makes his sign ("I felt it was going forth to conquer the only thing that mattered to me, sign and dominion and name").

Unfortunately, a spiteful contemporary named Kgwgk erases Qfvfq's sign and replaces it with his own. In a rage, Qfvfq wants "to make a new sign in space, a real sign that would make Kgwgk die of envy." So, out of competitiveness art is born. But the task of sign-making is becoming more difficult because the world "was beginning to produce an image of itself, and in everything a form was beginning to correspond to a function" (a theme from *The Nonexistent Knight*) and "in this new sign of mine you could perceive the influence of our new way of looking at things, call it style if you like. . . ."

Qfvfq is delighted with his new sign but as time passes he likes it less and less, thinks it is a bit pretentious, old-fashioned; decides he must erase it before his rival sees it (so writers revise old books or make new ones that obliterate earlier works—yes, call it style if you like). Finally, Qfvfq erases the inadequate sign. For a time he is pleased that there is nothing in space which might make him look idiotic to a rival—in this, he resembles so many would-be writers who contrive to vanish into universities and, each year, by not publishing that novel or poem, increase their reputations.

But doing nothing is, finally, abhorrent to the real artist: Qfvfq starts to amuse himself by making *false* signs, "to annoy Kgwgk . . . notches in space, holes, stains, little tricks that only an incompetent creature like Kgwgk could mistake for signs." So the artist masochistically mocks his own art, shatters form (the sign) itself, makes jokes to confuse and exploit 57th Street. But then things get out of hand. To Qfvfq's horror, every time he passes what he thinks was one of his false signs, there are a dozen other signs, all scribbled over his.

Finally, everything was now so obscured by a crisscross of meaningless signs that "world and space seemed the mirror of each other, both minutely adorned with hieroglyphics and ideograms" including "the badly inked tail of the letter *R* in an evening newspaper joined to a thready imperfection in the paper, one among the eight hundred thousand flakings of a tarred wall in the Melbourne docks. . . . In the universe now there was no longer a container and a thing contained, but only a general thickness of signs superimposed and coagulated."

Qfvfq gives up: there is no longer a point of reference "because it was clear that, independent of signs, space didn't exist and perhaps had never existed." So the story concludes: and the rest is the solipsism of art. To the old debate about being and nonbeing, Calvino adds his own vision of the multiplicity of signs which obliterates *all* meaning. Too many names for a thing is like no name for a thing, therefore, no thing, nothing.

"How Much Shall We Bet?" continues the theme. At the beginning Qfvfq "bet that there was going to be a universe, and I hit the nail on the head." This was the first bet he won with Dean (k)yK. Through the ages the two continue to make bets and Qfvfq usually wins because "I bet on the possibility of a certain event's taking place, whereas the Dean almost always bet against it."

Qfvfq kept on winning until he began to take wild leaps into the future. "On February 28, 1926, at Santhià, in Province of Vercelli—got that? At number 18 in Via Garibaldi—you follow me? Signorina Giuseppina Pensotti, aged twenty-two, leaves her home at quarter to six in the afternoon: does she turn right or left?" Qfvfq starts losing. Then they begin to bet about characters in unwritten novels . . . will Balzac make Lucien de Rubempré kill himself at the end of *Les illusions perdues*? The Dean wins that one.

The two betters end up in charge of vast research foundations which contain innumerable reference libraries. Finally, like man's universe itself, they begin to drown in signs and Qfvfq looks back nostalgically to the beginning, "How beautiful it was then, through that void, to draw lines and parabolas, pick out the precise point, the intersection between space and time when the event would spring forth, undeniable in the prominence of its glow; whereas now events come flowing down without interruption, like cement being poured, one column next to the other . . . a doughy mass of events without form or direction, which surrounds, submerges, crushes all reasoning."

In another story the last of the dinosaurs turns out to be Qfvfq who meets and moves in with the next race. The New Ones don't realize that he is one of their dread enemies from the past. They think him remarkably ugly but not unduly alien. Qfvfq's attitude is like that of the protagonist in William Golding's *The Inheritors* except that in Calvino's version the last of the Old Ones merges with the inheritors. Amused, Qfvfq listens to the monstrous, conflicting legends about his race, tribute to the power of man's imagination, to the words he uses, to the signs he recognizes.

Finally, "I knew that the more the Dinosaurs disappear, the more they extend their dominion, and over forests far more vast than those that cover the continents: in the labyrinth of the survivors' thoughts." But Qfvfq was not at all sentimental about being the last dinosaur and at the story's end he left the New Ones and "travelled through valleys and plains. I came to a station, caught the first train, and was lost in the crowd."

In "The Spiral," the last of the *Cosmicomics*, Qfvfq is a mollusk on a rock in the primeval sea. The theme is again *in ovo omnes*. Calvino describes with minuteness the sensations of the mollusk on the rock, "damp and happy. . . . I was what they call a narcissist to a slight extent; I mean I stayed there observing myself all the time, I saw all my good points and all my defects, and I liked myself for the former and for the latter; I had no terms of comparison, you must remember that, too." Such was Eden. But then the heat of the sun started altering things; there were vibrations from another sex; there were eggs to be fertilized: love.

In response to the new things, Qfvfq expresses himself by making a shell which turns out to be a spiral that is not only very good for defense but unusually beautiful. Yet Qfvfq takes no credit for the beauty: "My shell made itself, without my taking any special pains to have it come out one way rather than another." But then the instinctive artist in the mollusk asserts itself: "This doesn't mean that I was absent-minded during that time; I applied myself instead, to the act of secreting. . . ." Meanshile, *she*, the beloved, is making *her* shell, identical with his.

Ages pass. The shell-Qfvfq is on a railroad embankment as a train passes by. A party of Dutch girls looks out the window. Qfvfq is not startled by anything for, "I feel as if, in making the shell, I had also made the rest." But one new element has entered the equation. "I had failed to foresee one thing: the eyes that finally opened to see us didn't belong to us but to others." So dies Narcissus. "They developed eyes at our expense. So sight, *our* sight, which we were obscurely waiting for, was the sight that the others had of us."

But the artist who made the spiral-shaped shell is not to be outdone by miscalculation or by fate. Proudly he concludes: "All these eyes were mine. I had made them possible; I had had the active part; I furnished them the raw material, the image." Again the gallant coda, for fixed in the watcher's eye is not only the fact of the beautiful shell that *he* made but also "the most faithful image of her" who had inspired the shell and was the shell: thus male and female are at last united in the retina of a stranger's eye.

In 1967, Calvino published more of Qfvfq's adventures in *Time and the Hunter.* For the most part they are engaging cartoons, but one is disconcerted to encounter altogether too many bits of Sarraute, of Robbe-Grillet, of Borges (far too much of Borges) incorporated in the prose of what I have come to regard as a true modern master (*Pace* Kermode). On page 6 occurs "viscous"; on page 11 "acid mucus." I started to feel queasy: these are Sarraute words. I decided that their use was simply a matter of coincidence. But when, on page 29, I saw the dread word "magma" I knew that Calvino has been too long in Paris, for only Sarrautistes use "magma," a word the great theoretician of the old New Novel so arbitrarily and uniquely appropriated from the discipline of science. Elsewhere in the stories, Robbe-Grillet's technique of recording the minutiae of a banal situation stops cold some of Calvino's best effects.

   "The Chase," in fact, could have been written by Robbe-Grillet. This is not a compliment. Take the beginning:

> That car that is chasing me is faster than mine; inside there is one man, alone, armed with a pistol, a good shot. . . . We have stopped at a traffic signal, in a long column. The signal is regulated in such a way that on our side the red light lasts a hundred and eighty seconds and the green light a hundred and twenty, no doubt based on the premise that the perpendicular traffic is heavier and slower.

And so on for sixteen pages, like a movie in slow motion.

   The theory behind this sort of enervating prose goes like this: since to write is to describe, with words, why not then describe words themselves (with other words)? Or, glory be! words describing words describing an action of no importance (the corner of that room in Robbe-Grillet's *Jalousie*). This sort of "experiment" has always seemed to me to be of more use to students of language than to readers of writing. On his own and at his best, Calvino does what very few writers can do: he describes imaginary worlds with the most extraordinary precision and beauty (a word he has single-handedly removed from that sphere of suspicion which the old New Novelists used to maintain surrounds all words and any narrative).

   In *Cosmicomics* Calvino makes it possible for the reader to inhabit a meson, a mollusk, a dinosaur—makes him see for the first time light as it ends the dark universe. Since this is a unique gift, I find all the more alarming the "literariness" of *Time and the Hunter.* I was particularly put off by the central story "t zero," which could have been written (and rather better) by Borges.

With a bow and arrow, Qfvfq confronts a charging lion. In his head he makes an equation: Time zero is where he Qfvfq is; where the Lion—L_o is. All combinations of a series which may be finite or infinite pass through Q_o's head, exactly like the man before the firing squad in Borges's celebrated story. Now it is possible that these stories will appeal to minds more convergent than mine (students of mathematics, engineers, Young Republicans are supposed to think convergently while novelists, gourmets, and non-Christian humanists think divergently) but to me this pseudoscientific rendering of a series of possibilities is deeply boring.

But there are also pleasures in this collection. Particularly "The Origin of the Birds." "Now these stories can be told better with strip drawings than with a story composed of sentences one after the other." So the crafty Calvino by placing one sentence after another *describes* a strip cartoon and the effect is charming even though Qfvfq's adventure among the birds is not really a strip cartoon but the description of a cartoon *in words*.

The narrator's technique is like that of *The Nonexistent Knight:* he starts to draw a scene; then erases it the way Sister Theodora used to eliminate oceans and forests as she hurried her lovers to their inevitable rendezvous. Calvino also comes as close as any writer can to saying that which is sensed about creation but may not be put into words (or drawn in pictures).

"I managed to embrace in a single thought the world of things as they were and of things as they could have been, and I realized that a single system included all." In the arms of Or, the queen of the birds, Qfvfq begins to *see* that "the world is single and what exists can't be explained without. . . ." But he has gone too far. As he is about to say the unsayable, Or tries to smother him. But he is still able to blurt out, "There's no difference. Monsters and non-monsters have always been close to one another! What hasn't been continues to be. . . ." At that point, the birds expel him from their paradise; and like a dreamer rudely awakened, he forgets his vision of unity. "(The last strip is all photographs: a bird, the same bird in close-up, the head of the bird enlarged, a detail of the head, the eye. . . .)" It is the same eye that occurs at the end of *Cosmicomics*, the eye of—well, cosmic consciousness for those who recall that guru of a past generation, Dr. Richard M. Bucke.

Calvino ends these tales with his own "The Count of Monte Cristo." The problem he sets himself is how to get out of Château d'If. Faria keeps making plans and tunneling his way through an endless, exitless fortress. Dantès, on the other hand, broods on the nature of the fortress as well as on the various drafts of the novel that Dumas is writing. In some drafts, Dantès will escape and find a treasure and get revenge on his enemies. In other drafts, he suffers a different fate. The narrator contemplates the possiblities of escape by considering the way a fortress (or a work of art) is made. "To plan a book—or an escape—the first thing to know is what to exclude." This particular story is Borges at his very best and, taking into account the essential unity of the multiplicity of all things, one cannot rule out that Calvino's version of *The Count of Monte Cristo* by Alexandre Dumas is indeed the finest achievement of Jorge Luis Borges imagined by Italo Calvino.

Calvino's seventh and latest novel (or work or meditation or poem) *Invisible Cities* is perhaps his most beautiful work. In a garden sit the aged Kublai Khan and the young Marco Polo—Tartar emperor and Venetian traveler. The mood is sunset. Prospero is holding up for the last time his magic wand: Kublai Khan has sensed the end of his empire, of his cities, of himself.

Marco Polo, however, diverts the emperor with tales of cities that he has seen within the empire and Kublai Khan listens, searches for a pattern in Marco Polo's Cities and memory, Cities and desire, Cities and signs, Thin Cities, Trading Cities, Cities and eyes, Cities and names, Cities and the dead, Cities and the sky, Continuous Cities, Hidden Cities. The emporer soon determines that each of these fantastic places is really the same place.

Marco Polo agrees: "'Memory's images, once they are fixed in words, are erased,' Polo said." (So does Borges, repeatedly!) "'Perhaps I am afraid of losing Venice all at once, if I speak of it, or perhaps, speaking of other cities, I have already lost it, little by little.'" Again the theme of multiplicity and wholeness, "when every city," as Calvino wrote at the end of "The Watcher," "is the City."

Of all tasks, describing the contents of a book is the most difficult and in the case of a marvelous invention like *Invisible Cities*, perfectly irrelevant. I shall spare myself the labor; noting, however, that something wise has begun to enter the Calvino canon. The artist seems to have made a peace with the tension between man's idea of the many and of the one. He could now, if he wanted, stop.

Yet Calvino is obliged to go on writing just as his Marco Polo goes on traveling because

> he cannot stop; he must go on to another city, where another of his pasts awaits him, or something perhaps that had been a possible future of his and is now someone else's present. Futures not achieved are only branches of the past: dead branches.

"Journeys to relive your past?" was the Khan's question at this point, a question which could also have been formulated: "Journeys to recover your future?"

And Marco's answer was: "Elsewhere is a negative mirror. The traveler recognizes the little that is his, discovering the much he has not had and will never have."

Later, after more descriptions of his cities, Kublai Khan decides that "the empire is nothing but a zodiac of the mind's phantasms."

"On the day when I know all the emblems," he asked Marco, "shall I be able to possess my empire, at last?"

And the Venetian answered, "Sire, do not believe it. On that day you will be an emblem among emblems."

Finally, Kublai Khan recognizes that all cities are tending toward the concentric circles of Dante's hell.

He said: "It is all useless, if the last landing place can only be the infernal city, and it is there that, in ever-narrowing circles, the current is drawing us."

And Polo said: "The inferno of the living is not something that will be; if there is one, it is what is already here, the inferno where we live every day, that we form by being together. There are two ways to escape suffering it. The first is easy for many: accept the inferno and become such a part of it that you can no longer see it. The second is risky and demands constant vigilance and apprehension; seek and learn to recognize who and what, in the midst of the inferno, are not inferno, then make them endure, give them space."

During the last quarter century Italo Calvino has advanced far beyond his American and English contemporaries. As they continue to look for the place where the spiders make their nests, Calvino has not only found that special place but learned how himself to make fantastic webs of prose to which all things adhere. In fact, reading Calvino, I had the unnerving sense that I was also writing what he had written; thus does his art prove his case as writer and reader become one, or One.

ANGELA M. JEANNET

Italo Calvino's Invisible City

I have long wondered why nobody has yet written an overview of Italian literature with a title such as: *In Praise of the City*, so varied, and insistent, and moving is the homage paid by Italian writers to that form of human community in all of its guises. That hypothetical volume could not limit itself to literature alone, but would touch upon certain constants of Italian culture as well, the culture expressed by—let's say—Renaissance thinkers and artists as well as the culture that is embodied in any Italian gardener (professional or amateur) tending a well-ordered orchard in the shadow of Etruscan or Roman or thirteenth-century city walls.

Once again, as when exploring other themes, we find one name emerging in this context, and marking an important point of confluence in the development of crucial motifs in our tradition: Italo Calvino. *Invisible Cities* is only his most recent contribution to the topic, but it lends itself with uncanny specificity and timeliness to the writing of a chapter for the non-existent volume I mentioned before. *Invisible Cities* reminds us—if we could have forgotten it—that this contemporary writer's originality feeds successfully upon the whole Italian tradition through a very complex system of connections, a maze of channels and capillaries, detours and thoroughfares. As importantly, Calvino's own diverse themes and techniques find in it, more than ever, coherence and originality; and the City, a

From *Perspectives on Contemporary Literature* 3, no. 1 (1977). © 1977 by *Perspectives on Contemporary Literature*.

major presence throughout all of Calvino's writings, emerges from it as the keystone of that coherence, as well as a privileged creation of human consciousness, the most significant avatar of human experience.

From the time when Calvino was writing *The Path to the Nests of Spiders*, in 1948, as the author himself said in a preface he wrote for the 1964 edition of that same youthful book, what preoccupied him most was the relationship between human events (adventures, quests) and the locus of their unfolding, in other words, the definition and the exploration of human consciousness within a specific environment. In that first *récit*, war invaded the countryside and the mountains, spilling out of the city so familiar to the young narrator. But the dichotomy city/country one might have expected to see develop in Calvino's universe, perhaps along Pavesian lines, did not materialize at all. The human community, town or city, lived on within the individual consciousness of each character. It increasingly served as a backdrop for action all throughout the works of Calvino's maturity, and—as a matter of fact—it went wherever his character moved: to battlefields and to treetops, back to prehistory or in the present, since human life seemed to find significance only within a community whose ultimate embodiment was that special entity called "the city." Escape from the immediate contact with other human beings and their conventions, as was the case in a *conte philosophique*, *The Baron in the Trees* ultimately turned out to be a calculated effort to gain a more lucid perspective on the human community, to understand what makes it human, to watch more effectively over its precariousness and to help it endure. For around it lie the woods, the lairs of the wolves, and only a philosopher can manage to live and stand watch right on the invisible line separating the outside from the inside, the chaos of being from existence. Inevitably, Calvino's protagonists move toward a closer connection with the city, even Qfvfq, in *Cosmicomics*, where the creative power of the writer retraces the process whereby society developed. Later, in a group of short stories gathered under the title *Marcovaldo or The Seasons and the City*, the hero's nostalgia for nature and open spaces, his sensitivity to the changing seasons in a cityscape polluted by all kinds of objects and living things, make sense only within the context of an urban setting: that's Marcovaldo's habitat. A very Italian Calvino tells us that, ultimately, Nature is a creation of the urban dweller, a necessary term in the dialectic of human experience. Only in the light of Marcovaldo's reluctant grasp of this truth does Cosimo's earlier adventure, his retreat into an unorthodox meditating and mediating position, acquire its full significance.

In 1969, in a brief autobiography written as an appendix to the first edition of *The Castle of Crossing Paths*, the image of the city emerged as a central element and an essential dimension of Calvino's poetic universe, a consciously chosen protagonist. Calvino wrote in a reflective mood, mixing playful loftiness and virtuosity. His life was quickly sketched in terms of a "geographical neurosis" from which he suffered, and in terms of the cities that "held" him: San Remo "luxuriantly green, once, combining cosmopolitan and eccentric influences and the touchy diffidence of a rustic coarseness"; Torino "industrious and rational . . . where the streets used to stretch interminably, deserted because of the rarity of cars . . . [where he] moved along invisible diagonals connecting the sides of grey triangles"; and many other excellent cities he desultorily came to know; and finally Paris "a city encircled by forests of beech and birch . . . encircling in its turn the National Library" where rare texts are consulted by a Calvino duly armed with an I.D. card. Then, between 1969 and 1972, significantly, Calvino concurrently reworked *The Castle of Crossing Paths* and wrote *Invisible Cities*.

There is a short story "Paese infido" written in 1953, which marks an important moment in Calvino's fiction: it is the last narrative to emerge from the thematic world of the Resistance, and serves as a bridge between that original source of inspiration and the later Calvino. The writer had begun his career by trying his hand at retelling the story of adolescents discovering the world through the events of the Resistance. But, in 1953, the economy and the intensity of this short story testify to the increased skill and depth of the young writer, and to the distance he has covered since the writing of *The Path to the Nests of Spiders*. As we read how the young Resistance fighter straggles into a small town in search of a doctor to dress his wounds, and how he meets with hostility, cowardice, and betrayal, we become aware of some things which are unmistakably the mark of the greater Calvino: a tone that's tense and vibrating with utterly controlled energy, a diction attentive and precise, a playfulness and a sense of discovery which even danger, and inhumanity, and ever-present death cannot repress. The title itself, with the difficulty it presents to the translator, announces a theme of the more mature artist: "Paese" is more than "village" and less than "city," the original human community nestled on a hill in the middle of a little valley, surrounded by the woods out of which the tracked man emerges, a community with its back streets, its square, its church, priest, doctor, and school teacher, and families sitting around tables at noon with soup spoons in their hands. For the protagonist, the *paese* means mistrust—"Paese infido"—and treachery; its every object becomes a part of a deadly trap. But the unexpected help he receives suddenly, from people he never sees, transform the ill-boding human landscape into beneficent presence, richer and more ambiguous than its own idyllic and one-dimensional self, contemplated from the outside at the beginning of the story. The wall of a stable—which had seemed to be a dead-end—harbors a breach, the locked and shuttered houses shelter compassionate people, a little girl with an apple in her hand appears and informs him matter-of-factly of an escape plan. So, the man escapes, crosses a little stream to safety, and in the light-hearted mood brought about by the discovery of a surprising truth, thinks: "Every town . . . even the most hostile and inhuman, has two faces. There comes a time when you discover its good face which was there all along; only, you couldn't see it, and you didn't know hope was possible."

Thus, Calvino's meditation on what other authors have called, a bit pompously, the human condition, finds a focus and its own understated expression with the discovery of ambiguity in the relationship between the individual and the cohesive entity we call "society." However, the latter is consistently viewed by Calvino in concrete terms, as a specific construct by a specific group of human beings; not an abstraction, but a tightly-woven physical, emotional, and intellectual presence, with its own suggestive name. Surprises abound, as characters pursue trite or unusual activities in a world full of significant clues and contradictory messages, all leading to an elusive—and yet ultimately attainable and rewarding—coherence.

The pursuit of elusive truth is the thread that runs through Calvino's later works. His readers (and Calvino himself) have noticed that his works tend to alternate curiously between two modes: one, factual, unadorned, apparently in tune with a contemporary environment (physical, mental, and emotional); the other, imaginative, rich in fantasy and humor and surprise. Teresa de Lauretis focused on the alternation defining it as "not a contradictory impasse but rather a dialectic process reflecting [Calvino's] awareness of the very nature of culture as the highest and unique form of human 'doing.'" The perceptiveness of de Lauretis' analysis is confirmed by an instance that is relevant to our topic, the development on two levels of the theme of the City, in two works that are very closely connected. The first—published in 1963—is a spare, matter-of-fact announcement of the theme, and the other is a development of that theme.

In *The Watcher,* a voting poll watcher (in Italian *scrutatore,* etymologically related to *scrutare* which mean "to observe closely and intently"), in order to perform his modest civic function, has to remain all day within the walls of a famous Italian sanatorium for the deformed, the Cottolengo, in Turin. Curiously enough, that same year 1953 which had seen Calvino's best effort to bring to full fruition the experience of the Resistance (an experience which was not only political, but psychological and intellectual also) had also seen the last attempt to exorcise what Calvino calls "le memorie difficili," the half-forgotten and yet haunting and painful memories of a youth's life *before* the Resistance, scenes of life in the country—an unfamiliar, unsettling reality—and of a stint in the Fascist youth organization at the beginning of

World War II. "L'entrata in guerra" contained a passage which pointed to the laboring of Calvino's imagination around the themes of the human community and its inherent ambiguities. A new, seminal element appeared there: the emergence of a secret and repugnant face of human groups, a literal revelation of deformity. When, because of some extraordinary event, a human community—mountain village, *paese*, or city—is forced to leave its accustomed shelters and habits, it displays to the outsider's horrified look the monsters it had kept hidden; soon, however, it regroups, and painfully regains its old equilibrium, as a disturbed insect settles in a new hiding place to show again only an iridescent shell, after desperately exposing pincers, legs, and soft underbelly to the fascinated eye of an intruder.

> Around us the refugees were busy transforming the classrooms into a labyrinth of village alleys, spreading sheets and hanging them on ropes for privacy, nailing shoe soles, washing stockings and hanging them up to dry, pulling out of their bags fried zucchini flowers and stuffed tomatoes, and looking for each other, counting heads, losing and recovering their stuff.
>
> But the peculiar characteristic of this bunch of humanity, the discontinuous theme which constantly recurred and first met your eye—as, when you enter a ballroom, you first see only the breasts and the shoulders of the ladies with the lowest decolletages—was the presence among them of cripples, goitered idiots, bearded women, dwarfs; it was the lips and noses deformed by lupus; it was the defenseless gaze of those affected by *delirium tremens*; it was the dark face of the mountain villages now forced to expose itself, to parade around; the old secrets of the peasant families, around which the village houses tighten like scales on a pinecone. Now, driven out of their dark lairs, they were trying again to find a hiding place, a balance, within the bureaucratic whiteness of those walls.
>
> In one of the classrooms the old people had all sat down at the desks. A priest also had appeared, and women were already clustering around him; he joked with them, gave them a bit of encouragement, and quivering smiles of trapped rabbits would flit on their faces too. And yet, the more their camp vaguely acquired a village air, the more they felt mutilated and scattered.

While the observer in the early *récit* was a teenager—a marginal presence in the flurry of war-related activites—in *The Watcher* the reflecting consciousness is a young man, intense and vaguely disillusioned, observant in a manner that suggests a questing mind, however sceptical and cautious, and a desire to grasp the secret sense of life: "Now he looked for something else in books: the wisdom of the ages, or simply something that would help him to understand something. The polling place which in an early "enlightened" mood he had viewed as "a dreariness . . . rich in signs and meanings perhaps even conflicting with one another," reveals itself significant beyond expectation, the center of a world unto itself, of a human community obeying its own rules, like a monstrous reverse of the everyday world familiar to the watcher and his colleagues. The sanatorium turns out to be the hidden face of the Piedmont region, the inside of that outside, the unseen twin city of industrious Turin, a city of human deformity. And yet, something essential about the very presence of the city is revealed to the thoughtful watcher. The significance of that entity: "a city" appears more clear and powerful as he looks—repelled and yet fascinated—at its counterpart, its grotesque caricature. The story—a mere 90 pages—is so close to historical events (1953 in Italy, one of the first elections after the war, a Communist intellectual properly ambivalent in his stances, too aware of contradictions and ambiguities, and very *philosophe* in the eighteenth-century sense of the word) that it reads and feels and moves along—apparently—like a documentary. But that understated, direct style is the finest disguise used by Calvino. The utter control exerted by the writer lies concealed all throughout, in the vocabulary and in the constructions of the masterfully structured text. The telling of that episode in the life of a man leaves us on a note so high, right at the end, that only another book, written after nine more years of experience, could exhaust it. As night falls on the Cottolengo courtyard, and some of the inmates scurry about playfully performing all kinds of chores, the watcher thinks: "Even the city of ultimate imperfection has its perfect moment . . . there is a time, an hour, when in any single city the City lives."

The day Calvino spent at the Cottolengo (at least in his imagination) was a fruitful one. His encounter with unfamiliar beings living on the threshold between humanity and non-humanity caused him to probe deeper into the modes of human relationships and into the significance of political and personal commitments. As we read *Invisible Cities—The Watcher's* chronologically distant twin work—we realize fully how charged the soft-spoken prose of *The Watcher* really was, and how crucial in Calvino's development. With *Invisible Cities,* we move from the contemporary to the fabulous, without losing the historical dimension. A questioning listener is addressed by a travelling stranger: the former is a Tartar conqueror, Kublai Khan, whose power is subtly undermined by his own restless wonderings, the latter is Marco Polo whose journeys (or imaginings?) yield marvelous tales. The setting is exotic, the names lend at the same time remoteness and flexibility to the text. A framework enclosing the series of reports Marco Polo makes to the Khan his patron develops the theme of melancholy meditation on the human condition. The aura of wonder and awe surrounding early explorations, legendary empires, and ancient Middle and Far Eastern tales is evoked with fastidious restraint. Static in his opulent gardens, surrounded by the wonders of a fabled court, the lonely Khan inquires about the world he possesses. His most reliable connection to that elusive outside is Marco the wayfarer whose path weaves repetitive patterns from the outside to the inside of their continuous dialogue. Marco Polo's reports are the reports of a new kind of *voyeur* or *scrutatore*, consistently an outsider but attentive to the minutest detail, master of the dizzying perspectives which allow him to capture totally and instantly the object of his obsession. One could say, as reviewers and critics have said, that Marco Polo's storytelling reinterprets the same human universe that had inspired a Boccaccio, a Chaucer, or an Ariosto, and that the *école du regard* and semiotics, Borges and Barthes preside over this re-interpretation. That would be an accurate, and yet misleading, statement. The prolific abandon, the wealth of space available in the earlier writers are not to be found here; nor do we have here the inhuman fixity of the objectified world of the *nouveau roman*. The story teller magnificently evokes the living presence of each city out of an empty space, desert or blank page. There is no other connective material to the tales than the measured dialogue between Marco and the Khan—voices speaking almost to themselves—no landscapes or digressions, secondary plots or characters. The connection between the reports is an internal one, a matter of structural relatedness by which each city, concretely seen, touched, and felt, is the singular manifestation of one City, ideal model and invisible inner coherence. Marco's passion and the Khan's disillusionment—on the other hand—invest the cities totally; the cities live within them. Calvino is clearly our contemporary, but he is also our *voyant*. Our recognition of intellectual interests we hold in common with him (structuralism and semiotics, for example) is accompanied by the awareness that for Calvino such interests become keys to a subtler understanding of his own (and our) poetic and cultural universe, and of the relationship between the two. His cities are not empty labyrinths.

Within the desert that surrounds them all, the cities are oases and market places, fair grounds and construction sites. The wealth of disparate elements and suggestions and recalls used by Calvino is impressive. Inside the limits of the cities, humanity lives, gesturing and speaking, bartering and telling tales, loving and killing, cooking and bathing, creating and destroying, touching and imagining, using in ever new combinations all the possible components of human experience. Yet, the potential infinity of those combinations is not overwhelming, because the narrator carefully weaves into his portraits the coherence presiding over the unity of the living city: whether dreamed or remembered, made up of precious stones or drowning in garbage, geometrically drawn or mushrooming without any plan, reflecting civic harmony or strife, each city is a manifestation of a common yearning. There is a City, the One that subsumes them all, and yet it is not an archetype. It lives in the here and now, in the multiplicity of actual cities which presuppose the ideal, and constantly recreate it. For Marco Polo, as the Khan discovers, the One is Venice, lost, remembered, and perhaps recaptured—Venice the beloved, and also Clarice (or Rome?), Leonia (or Milan?), Zirma (or New York?), Penthesilea (or Los Angeles?); the city omnipresent and unique, where the eye and the ear and the hand operate. Outside its limits, one can hear the wolves howl.

Cities and memory, cities and desire, cities and signs, cities and trade, thin cities and continuous cities, cities and eyes, cities and names, cities and the dead, cities and the sky, and then, hidden cities: one could play interminably with the potential clusters of pairs suggested by the text, and with references to the obvious sources of Calvino's categories. However, everything is subsumed by the title of the collection, *Invisible Cities* since those cities are eminently concrete and yet invisible, and the imagination alone, mobile and ever-productive, can see them. Invisible cities, because the world of human experience needs a perceptive interpreter, who will see between the lines—so to speak—who will detect in transparency what is hidden, remnant of the past or blueprint for the future, powerful yet secret statement; and because each of them contains, inevitably, the reverse of its visible traits, and that invisible negative also contributes to the city's presence, makes it dynamic and human. Thus, Zaira carries inscribed within its present all of its past; Zora—the city that died—lives in human memory as a mnemonic device; and Despina lives in terms of the twin loneliness of sea and desert, where men dreamed of the city; and Marsilia—all new—lives in the shadow of a ghostly city made up of old photographs; and Armilla's only physical reality is a landscape of waterpipes inhabited by a delightfully contemporary breed of water nymphs; and Ottavia is a city suspended over a gorge, an intricate swaying net loaded with the paraphernalia of everyday life; and Bauci is the absent city contemplating its own absence from the top of immense pileworks; and Berenice, the unjust city, hides within itself the city of the just which in turn harbors the seeds of the city of self-righteousness, the malignant seeds of injustice.

How do the cities of the Khan's empire live? In Marco Polo's narration. Since there are only two characters, and no plot at all, the cities are also the only adventure. The wealth of events to which our tradition of story-telling had accustomed us has been pared down to what is ultimately of greatest importance to Calvino: the multiplicity of human invention, as embodied in the cities. The Kublai Khan has conquered lands, and now doubts the very existence of his kingdom; Marco Polo has "seen" those lands, and now brings back the evidence of the human presence in this world. His tale of fifty-five cities means reassurance and discovery. In this *dédoublement* of human experience, as Kublai Khan and Marco Polo, as action and creative imagining, Calvino reaffirms the validity of human endeavor in a present which—although contemplated with a certain stoic pensiveness—is not haunted by metaphysical dreams or metaphysical nightmares. The techniques used to help the listener to "discern, through the walls and towers destined to crumble, the tracery of a pattern so subtle it could escape the termites' gnawing" (*Invisible Cities*, tr. by William Weaver) have attracted a lot of attention, because of their novelty, and because of their complex inter-weaving. They also serve to develop two other themes: the theme of the game and the theme of human expression. In brief: there are nine sections to the volume. The first and the last contain the portraits of ten cities each. The other seven sections contain only five portraits each, for a total of fifty-five cities that comprise the major part of the volume. Eighteen passages serve as preface and epilogue to each section. Within this outline, the cities fall, five by five, under eleven different headings, in such a manner that one heading is added at every turn, and one of them is dropped after its fifth appearance. It's not the first time that Calvino has played elaborate games in his texts; even in *The Watcher*, factual as it appeared to be, Amerigo Ormea's name suggested a penchant toward playfulness. But the *divertissement* is now painstakingly integrated in the overall plan of the work; the game is serious, more ambitious. The persona Calvino has chosen, Marco Polo-Kublai Khan, although given to whimsy, is a mature human being in his age of reflection. Under the conventions of different games—the combinations of series of numbers, the patters of poems and stories, of sounds and letters, the moves on a chessboard, the rules of card playing, all ancient means used by humanity to discover meaning and order in chaos—the writer is pursuing analogies and echoes, underlying currents and fixed points, the rules that control and constrain and make sense out of the infinitely varied reality of human expression and communication. Thus, the titles of the sections repeat a limited number of words in groups that suggest (or create, perhaps) hypnotically monotonous stanzas, as in a rigorously constructed poem: "Cities and memory, cities and memory, cities and desire, cities and memory, cities and desire, cities and signs." (*Invisible Cities*, Contents.) A, AB, ABC, ABCD, ABCDE, BCDEF, CDEFG, DEFGH, EFGHI, FGHIJ, GHIJK, HIJK, IJK, JK, K. And then the numerical sequences that enclose in rigid patterns a proliferation of possibilities: 1; 2,1; 3,2,1; then 5,4,3,2,1 repeated seven times; and then 5,4,3,2; 5,4,3; 5,4; 5. The word pattern carefully contradicts (and therefore reinforces) the numerical pattern.

However, the game would be shallow, if one were to describe it solely in formal terms. This reticulation of numbers and letters is intimately connected to other, less obvious patterns, and it is only through the total effort that an elusive truth is captured. Once again, the formalized games yield a secret, that "invisibility" which Marco is able to interpret and verbalize: through the intricate pattern of numbers, words, lines, and blank spaces Calvino is hunting for the food that feeds another human hunger, the need to make sense out of the world. The sterile chessboard, which the Khan is tempted to see as the maze where meaningless moves are made, ruled by Chance, leading to nothingness, becomes for Marco a theatre of events, reflecting totally human passion and ingenuity, rich in symbols and signs, structured by rules of order under the apparent randomness, a perfect portrait of crafty imagination, and a mirror of action. Even the wood out of which the chessboard is made reveals to the eye of the seer the fascinating history of the world.

One is reminded at this point of Calvino's earler text, *The Castle of Crossing Paths;* there also, a game, the tarots, revealed its intrinsic potential as a system of signs which could be used for human communication, indeed which human beings had devised as another code to capture the variety and the color of their experiences. But in *Invisible Cities* other preoccupations have become Calvino's primary concern. The framework surrounding the several groupings of cities is important in this context, since it contains the dialogue between Marco Polo and the Khan, and follows a very precise pattern. The Khan is a sceptical listener, and Marco Polo is able to arouse his curiosity by a game of pantomime; by-passing the spoken word of which he pretends at first to be ignorant, he makes use of a different code (which the writer, we suppose, transcribes). Later, we learn that, unlike the travellers of *The Castle of Crossing Paths,* Marco is not at all unskilled in the Khan's language, but has simply judged that the common code of communication has become tired or suspect. The Khan would not listen, perhaps, to a familiar pattern of sounds; Marco's pantomime, subject to several interpretations, ambiguous and sensuous, engages his attention, hence elicits his participation in the creative process. Dreams also are a valid code, but from the number of conceivable dreams one "must exclude those whose elements are assembled without a connecting thread, an inner rule, a perspective, a discourse." (*Invisible Cities.*) The task of the storyteller, then, is to bring to light the hidden face of the dream or of the city, the intimate links, the secret structures that support what is visible in human expression. That's why the sixth section speaks of the journey as illusory movement. The mind lives and relives all the dreams of humankind in its meditative moments, and detects their intimate logic within their surprising diversity. There is a most dangerous temptation, as we learn from the Khan's experience, a temptation that Marco Polo, who is the disciplined imagination, rightly rejects: that is to follow the narrower and narrower circles of the speculating mind, the empty rigor and grace of the game, the disconnected features of the inhuman city. Seated by the chessboard, Kublai Khan recognized within the game of the chess the rules underlying all the other games, but the goal of the game has escaped him. "The end of every game is a gain or a loss; but of what? (*Invisible Cities*.)

Ultimately, the text is a celebration of three of the richest systems of signs and symbols devised by humans: the City, the Game, and the Word, in all of their complexity, ambiguity, and promise for human exchange. Cities, games, and stories emerge from parallel semantic codes, tightly related and perfectly analogous; language is the ideal medium to speak the city which lives in a concrete environment made up of climate, location, seasons, colors, sounds, smells, gestures, dreams, ideals. Cities are like volumes with written pages, like stories told by imaginative and well-travelled tellers, and games played by gambler-philosophers. The City with a capital "c" is to the innumerable cities what the *langue* is to the *parole* (poem or tale), and what the Game with a big "g" is to the innumerable games. None of the objects designated by a word with a capital letter exists of and by itself, each lives only in the actual plurality of the statements uttered, of the games played, of the cities built. Calvino, as the writer he is, the specific writer he is, knows that to say "city" is to speak. In history and in fiction, the city is also a literary entity, the locus of an ideal, of a desire, of a remembrance, an invisible presence not unlike the heroines whose names we know by heart; so, his cities are called, with female names, Diomira, Isidora, Dorothea, Zaira, Anastasia, Tamara, Zora, Despina . . . They live on within the human consciousness: "Cities . . . believe they are the work of the mind or of chance, but neither the one nor the other suffices to hold up their walls. You take delight not in a city's seven or seventy wonders, but in the answer it gives to a question of yours. Or the question it asks you, forcing you to answer, like Thebes through the mouth of the Sphinx" (*Invisible Cities*.)

It has been pointed out that the contemporary city, with its frightening growth and its many forms of decay, and the cities that "menace in nightmares and maledictions" (*Invisible Cities*) are very present in Calvino's work. Again, the voices of the writer's personae remind us of the problematic position we are in vis-à-vis our life in this world. Without ponderousness or sentimentality, in a meditative and firm tone, they restate what the earlier Calvino had sensed. The Khan says: "It is all useless, if the last landing place can only be the infernal city, and it is there that, in ever-narrowing circles, the current is drawing us." And the man who is rich in experience and insight, the restless Venetian yearning for and fleeing from his beloved city responds: "The inferno of the living is not something that will be; if there is one, it is what is already here, the inferno where we live every day, that we form by being together. There are two ways to escape suffering it. The first is easy for many: accept the inferno and become such a part of it that you can no longer see it. The second is risky and demands constant vigilance and apprehension: seek and learn to recognize who and what, in the midst of the inferno, are not inferno, then make them endure, give them space."

Such is the quest Marco Polo embarked upon. The invisible is made visible, the visible is pushed aside to allow us other, more important discoveries. Calvino's language, with its at times subtle but more often sudden changes of register, and with its diverse references, is the most adept tool for this enterprise. This is an author who truly lives in a world from which no one voice of the past is absent, and to which no human experience—but despair—is denied access.

TERESA DE LAURETIS

Semiotic Models, Invisible Cities

What is the city?
It is a place in the sand where a field of energy
keeps the octagonal silicate crystals in perfect order,
lined axis end to axis end. . . . Responding to the
psychic pressures of those who observed it, at times
the city seemed a lake, at others a catacombe of
caves. Once it had appeared a geyser of flame, and
occasionally it looked like buildings, towers, looped
together with elevated roads, with double light
glinting from thousands of sunward windows.
                    Samuel R. Delany, *The Fall of the Towers*

In his book on the poetics of the open work, Umberto Eco pointed out the design, explicit in the "project" of the contemporary art work, to use techniques of discontinuity and indetermination for the purpose of generating open series of performances or interpretations by the reader/listener/viewer: "we note [in the work] the tendency to ensure that every performance of the work will never coincide with an ultimate definition of it; every performance realizes the work but all performances are complementary to one another; finally, every performance renders the work in a complete and satisfying manner but at the same time also renders it incomplete" ⟨*Opera aperta*, my

From *Yale Italian Studies* (Winter 1978). © 1978 by *Yale Italian Studies*.

translation). Whether the death of criticism, already predicted to follow the death of the novel and of the logocentric civilization, will occur during this century is a problem of small practical importance. What must be invented, if criticism is to continue to be useful for the time being, is a way to cope with what's at hand, a critical language to account for the works of (narrative) literature being produced now, an informed and imaginative approach to works— experimental or not—whose project is to subvert the accepted literary codes and genres, and to redefine the parameters of esthetic communication.

By this, I do not mean to imply that the critical activity is a secondary or parasitic effort with regard to the so-called creative activity. On the contrary, criticism has equal claim to the resources of the imagination, to invention, to the continual reshaping of our cultural reality. In fact, if literature and criticism have always been engaged in a relation of mutual feedback, they seem to be even more so in the current interdisciplinary climate when criticism, while demanding recognition of its independent worth and creative freedom, is also much more conscious of its social implications and capacity for theoretical work. In turn, literature reflects the critical and speculative mood of the times, however indirectly. For representation in contemporary literature is all but mimetic or naive, and rather than with reality its concern is with the conditions and mechanisms of representation itself. The object and the mode of most contemporary narrative merge in the attempt to represent not reality but the perception of it, not the world but epistemology, not the fantasy but the dreamwork—in other words, not existents or essences but relations and processes.

The work, Eco also suggests, is an epistemological metaphor, an autonomous form which places itself side by side with the existing scientific and cultural forms through which the world is perceived, understood, known. And, in every period or culture, the ways in which art forms are structured and produced reflect (again, indirectly) that particular historical view of the world. If Eco is right, then the work already implies various extratextual epistemological models of its time including literary models such as the genres, broadly defined, or works by other authors, contemporary or not, as Cervantes and Don Quijote are to Pierre Menard, are to Borges. These models, however, are not to be understood as "models imitated" by the author or "models inherent in the logic of the work" (as a structural model might be). To do so would close the work, give a complete, airtight, nondialectic view of it. Rather, I would argue, these models are formative influences whose "anxiety" the author is precisely attempting, successfully or not, to deal with. At the same time, the critic also is influenced by extratextual models: does it matter whether the two sets of models, the artist's and the critic's, coincide? I think not. This is one more reason why the critical discourse makes the reader aware that those models which may be seen projected into or reflected out of the work are historical, in the sense of culture bound, period-specific, and not explicative but rather *implicative*. This is to say they do not explain the work but, on the contrary, build further implications into it, and are interpretants in the Peircian sense— signs or sign systems used to translate a discourse into another, to transform the first text into a second text, one code into a different code. By offering several different (but not randomly chosen) models, criticism can suggest possible paths of reading, translating, reorganizing, making sense of, and interpreting the text without imposing a single center of perspective or constraining the text into one closed set or frame of reference. The critic can, in this manner, open the text to the extratextual, to cultural reality, and still render it incomplete and expose the critical discourse itself as a new assemblage of semiotic possibilities.

In this essay I am going to look at a contemporary narrative text, Italo Calvino's *Invisible Cities*, to try to explore the rules that, whether followed or broken, underlie its composition or "project," and some of the codes through which the critical discourse becomes possible. I will present and discuss three models for the study of narrative fiction and relate them to Calvino's text: the model elaborated by the structural analysis of narrative (from Propp to Lévi-Strauss to Barthes), a model proposed by the Soviet semiotician Jury Lotman, and a Freudian model. My purpose is not only to speculate on the work of Calvino but also to raise questions as to the notions of narrative text, open or closed work, and representation in contemporary literature, and ultimately to attempt to identify the by-ways of the literary imagination and to show that they can not be separated from the paths of the critical imagination.

II

Kublai Khan does not necessarily believe everything Marco Polo says when he describes the cities visited on his expeditions, but the emperor of the Tartars does continue listening to the young Venetian with greater attention and curiosity than he shows any other messenger or explorer of his. In the lives of emperors there is a moment which follows pride in the boundless extension of the territories we have conquered, and the melancholy and relief of knowing we shall soon give up any thought of knowing and understanding them. There is a sense of emptiness that comes over us at evening, with the odor of the elephants after the rain and the sandalwood ashes growing cold in the braziers. . . . It is the desperate moment when we discover that this empire, which had seemed to us the sum of all wonders, is an endless, formless ruin, that corruption's gangrene has spread too far to be healed by our scepter, that the triumph over enemy sovereigns has made us the heirs of their long undoing. Only in Marco Polo's accounts was Kublai Khan able to discern, through the walls and towers destined to crumble, the tracery of a pattern so subtle it could escape the termites' gnawing. (*Invisible Cities*, tr. by William Weaver)

As in traditional narratives, the opening sets the stage for the story's unfolding, as one used to say or, perhaps better, presents signals or traces of the possible worlds within the discourse of the text: *a dialogue* of two voices speaking across the space of continents, from the beginning of one civilization to the end of another. The space has been collapsed in discourse, however, and the Tartars' Empire duplicates the western empire now at its breaking point; then, *Marco Polo's accounts*, récits of his travels, descriptions of cities of the mind, places where only the imagination has been or will be—the tense does not matter to the imagination; and then, *a pattern like a filigree*, so delicate and subtle and immaterial, yet perceptible, discernible—but where? In what order of reality, in what processes of mind, by what human senses?

Cities also believe they are the work of the mind or of chance, but neither the one nor the other suffices to hold up their walls. You take delight not in a city's seven or seventy wonders, but in the answer it gives to a question of yours.

What question shall we ask of the text? The first and most obvious one elicited by *Invisible Cities* is: how can one describe what one does not see? Or, which is the same question, how can a filigree be *so* fine as to escape the termites' gnawing? To answer this question is to pass to another order of reality, to function by metaphor, to subsume the concrete object in its representation, to enter the discursive or symbolic order, to place ourselves in the process of semiosis. And immediately another question presents itself: is the whole text nothing but a question-producing mechanism? And, if so, are all texts question-producing mechanisms?

Calvino's is an open text, that is to say a question-producing mechanism, an ambiguous multilevel message that exposes the contradictions internal to its own system and to the cultural codes it assumes rather than a closed text, which is an answer-producing mechanism, a device used to resolve contradictions, to pacify the intellect, to reaffirm—however indirectly—the inevitability or cultural patterns, the presumed presence and order of the world. One can say that the openness of the open work is internal to it, is inherent in its formal organization, as is the closedness of the closed work. This does not mean that only open works are esthetic objects, or that any open text is good literature. I use the terms "open" and "closed" descriptively and in reference to specific historical esthetic factors that accompany the production of literary objects.

Model 1. Structural analysis has shown that narrative discourse has its own formal rules, and that these rules are followed, consciously and unconsciously, by anyone who originates or repeats or summarizes a narrative, regardless of its content, or the narrator's culture or natural language. In other words, there is a logic of narrative, a transcultural narrative pattern, and the pattern itself has a meaning. Moreover, that meaning is not itself a content or a set of values, but it may be used to reinforce values, assumptions, and expectations, as it may be used to question them or to destroy them. The power inherent in the knowledge of the existence of such meaning lies in the fact that, because of its formal, immaterial, and intangible nature, the meaning of the pattern is not immediately perceived by the readers/listeners/viewers, and therefore can be used to manipulate them. *Invisible Cities* is an open work in the sense that it challenges the narrative pattern itself, exposing its meaning, its logic, its power. In order to do so, Calvino's discourse must replace the usual organization of narrative elements with another form of organization, a different and more subtle pattern. The accounts of Marco Polo's journeys and the descriptions of cities are common elements of two narrative genres, the adventure story and the book of travels (beginning with the *Odyssey* and, of course, the real Marco Polo's *Il milione*). But *Invisible Cities*, in fact, contains no action or characters in the usual sense of the term, no real events or adventures, and the travels themselves are never depicted. The cities described are not related to one another geographically or by historical chronology but only, if at all, by an invisible thread which exists somewhere in Marco Polo's memory, or rather in his discourse. The dialogue frame enveloping the storytelling is typical of a worldwide narrative type that includes works like *The Thousand and One Nights, Decameron, Canterbury Tales*, Basile's *Pentamerone*, and collections of folk and literary tales, and that probably has its genesis in the communal myth- and story-telling gatherings from which ritual and theater also originated. Calvino's book does reflect the number systems generally imposed on such collections and consists of multiples of a given number (for example, ten days, ten narrators, 100 stories in *Decameron*). This recurs also in epic and heroic poems, in the numerology of the *Divine Comedy*, in metric forms, and so forth. But Calvino's distribution of the cities in eleven categories, each of which is repeated five times, appears to be a random one, where numbers and categories have no allegorical meaning, no logical or symbolic necessity. In this manner the magic of the number pattern is exposed as convention. However, if we compare *Invisible Cities* with other books of his like *Il Castello dei destini incrociati*, it is evident that the pattern here is even more than a number game in the way of mathematical combinatory possibilities, and more than a tongue-in-cheek commentary on the old genres. That in this work the number pattern also fulfills a semiotic function of the system-text can be seen considering another model.

Model 2. According to Lotman, two semiotic models are available in constructing narratives: the syntagmatic combination of elements in space, by which the text increases in size by the addition of new words, sentences, paragraphs, chapters (the typical mechanism of verbal narration and the primary semiotic system on which verbal narration is based, i.e., natural language); and the transformation of an initial "stable state" into another by the rearrangement of its internal elements, and the subsequent combination in time. In this type of text, which Lotman calls *iconic*, the signs and sign series of the *discrete* verbal narrative are replaced by pictorial segments, each of which is synchronically organized like a picture, a figure. The segments do not join in space but "are transformed one into another, becoming a summation in time" ("The Discrete Text and the Iconic Text"). In the iconic, nondiscrete text, narration is a transformation, an internal transposition of elements, as are the figures obtained in a kaleidoscope. While painting is the obvious starting point of the iconic text for its "initial stage," the model of its syntagmatic development is provided by music, which is development of movement in its pure, nonsemantic form.

> In this sense, the film narrative (especially in the silent film) represents a fuller form of the iconic narrative text as it combines the semantic essence of painting with the transformational syntagmatic quality of music. However, the question would be simple, or even primitive, if this or that art were automatically to realize the constructive possibilities of its material. And it is not a question, either, of "mastering the material" as the formalists understood it.

The relationship is more complex; it is a question of freedom vis-à-vis the material, of those acts of conscious artistic choice that can either preserve the structure of the material or violate it. . . . As a consequence, verbal narrative is a revolutionizing element in immanently iconic narration, and vice versa.

Going back to Calvino, the text of *Invisible Cities* is both iconic and discrete: the description of each city is a stable state, an iconic system, a pictorial representation of objects, volumes, and relations. Each successive city is a transformation of a previous one obtained by transposition of its formal and essentially mobile elements.

Kublai Khan had noticed that Marco Polo's cities resembled one another, as if the passage from one to another involved not a journey but a change of elements. Now, from each city Marco described to him, the Great Khan's mind set out on its own, and after dismantling the city piece by piece, he reconstructed it in other ways, substituting components, shifting them, inverting them.

As a result, what Lotman calls the " summation in time" of the narrative is a cinematic effect of fade-ins, fade-outs or dissolves from one image into another into another. . . . The syntagmatic sequence of the images, interspersed with fragments of the circular dialogue between Marco Polo and Kublai Khan, has the movement of a fugue: 55 sections (the cities) each containing one of eleven different and recurring motifs or musical phrases (e.g., cities and memory, thin cities, cities and the dead, etc.) spaced unevenly across the nine parts of the composition (the nine chapters of the narrative), and each part is preceded and followed by connective "bars" of dialogue. Instead of grouping the cities by motif or category, as in the classical tale collections, and thus constraining the possible transformations of each structure within a thematic norm, Calvino disperses the eleven categories throughout the nine chapters, giving the *impression* of an open generative process. That the arrangement is in fact not random, one can discover by studying the table of contents where a mathematical pattern soon becomes visible. But Calvino does have his cake and eat it too because he creates the impression of random or free generation of the images while in fact imposing an order which is itself not necessary but pure play.

By superimposing the iconic and the musical modes of textual organization upon the discrete verbal narrative (which is itself imposed upon the primary system of natural language), Calvino produces a discourse that can not be spoken because it is essentially *écriture*, written text, esthetic object, almost a form of conceptual art. *Invisible Cities* is then a work that challenges the accepted narrative pattern, and this is one way of disintegrating the logic of narrative, of provoking and sustaining questions in the reader. There is yet another, more subtle design in the text, the intentional and ideological act of the writer that Ihab Hassan would call "the will to unmaking." To illustrate this, let us consider another model, another game we all have played.

Model 3. In a short paper written in 1924 entitled "A Note upon the 'Mystic Writing-Pad'" (*Notiz über den Wunderblock*, which would have been translated better as "magic" writing-pad), Freud describes a contrivance, usually sold as a toy, consisting of a wax slab covered by a partly detachable cellophane sheet. He notes that the device combines the two characteristics of the human perceptual apparatus, unlimited receptive capacity and retention or permanent memory traces. Despite the fact that, once the writing has been erased by lifting the covering sheet the magic pad cannot reproduce it from within, this toy is an excellent concrete metaphor of the human mind where stimuli remain permanently recorded in the unconscious (the wax slab) even when they have been erased from consciousness (the covering sheet). Freud concludes:

> If we imagine one hand writing upon the surface of the . . . pad while another periodically raises its covering-sheet from the wax slab, we shall have a concrete representation of the way in which I tried to picture the functioning of the perceptual apparatus of our mind.

Calvino writes as on a Wunderblock, constantly raising the covering sheet after the inscription of each city, and inserting now and then a fragment of the dialogue between Marco Polo and Kublai Khan almost as if to recharge the imagination, to reestablish contact, to counter the "discontinuity in the current of innervation." The cities, and their descriptions, are inevitably discontinuous, each being a self-consistent system, a form. But the narrative construction is a process, both for the writer and for the reader; narration, therefore, must provide a higher code, a rule that allows linking one city to another in a continuous and reversible process, countering the discontinuity of the syntagmatic chain by means of a paradigmatic continuity (Lotman's "summation in time") which is itself synchronic. In Calvino's text the diachronic discontinuity of verbal narrative (the description of the cities on the syntagmatic axis) and the synchronic continuity (on the paradigmatic axis) of affect, memory, and signification, constitute the dialectic (dialogue) of the communicative process.

In reallocating Freud's metaphor to Calvino's writing I only wish to show the functioning of the contemporary imagination, both critical and creative. If Freud wanted to make patterns and sense out of the irrational, unreasonable fictions of human desire, Calvino (I think) wants to deconstruct all ready-made patterns of meaning as well as (and I intend it literally) urban planning. But Freud and Calvino have essentially the same view of the mechanisms of fiction-making, of the functioning of the imagination and its constitutive, creative acts. The endless circulation of the signifier of desire in the text, and its continuous metonymic displacement in the representation of objects, cities, feelings, memories, visions which are the form and content of these "travels," stem from a primary *locus*, a mythical, archetypal city of mind—Venice.

After sunset, on the terraces of the palace, Marco Polo expounded to the sovereign the results of his missions. As a rule the Great Khan concluded his day savoring these tales with half-closed eyes until his first yawn was that signal for the suite of pages to light the flames that guided the monarch to the Pavilion of the August Slumber. But this time Kublai seemed unwilling to give in to weariness. "Tell me another city," he insisted.

". . . You leave there and ride for three days between the northeast and east-by-northeast winds. . . ." Marco resumed saying, enumerating names and customs and wares of a great number of lands. His repertory could be called inexhaustible, but now he was the one who had to give in. Dawn had broken when he said: "Sire, now I have told you about all the cities I know."

"There is still one of which you never speak."

Marco Polo bowed his head.

"Venice," the Khan said.

Marco smiled. "What else do you believe I have been talking to you about?"

The emperor did not turn a hair. "And yet I have never heard you mention that name."

And Polo said: "Everytime I describe a city I am saying something about Venice."

"When I ask you about other cities' qualities, I want to hear about them. And about Venice, when I ask you about Venice."

"To distinguish the other cities' qualities, I must speak of a first city that remains implicit. For me it is Venice."

"You should then begin each tale of your travels from the departure, describing Venice as it is, all of it, not omitting anything you remember of it."

> The lake's surface was barely wrinkled; the copper reflection
> of the ancient palace of the Sung was shattered into sparkling
> glints like floating leaves.

Marco Polo's city of origin has no referent in reality and exists only in its
varying representations, the different signifiers of his discourse like shattered
reflections on the water, in an open series of subsequent but not progressive
approximations.

The form of expression of the work is mirrored in the form of content
of each city, for all of Marco Polo's cities are metaphors of absence: Isidora,
the city one dreams of in one's youth but can reach only in one's old age;
Fedora, the stone metropolis which contains, in small crystal globes, "the
forms the city could have taken if, for one reason or another, it had not
become what we see today"; Bauci, whose inhabitants live on stilts so high
they reach the clouds and from where "with spyglasses and telescopes aimed
downward they never tire of examining it, leaf by leaf, stone by stone, ant by
ant, contemplating with fascination their own absence"; or Clarice, for which
"the order of the eras' succession has been lost; that a first Clarice existed is
a widespread belief, but there are no proofs to support it." Tamara is a city
made of signs, of icons whose referents are forever lost, their ontological
essence unknowable, for behind the signs only interpretants may be found,
signs of other signs.

> You walk for days among trees and among stones. Rarely does
> the eye light on a thing, and then only when it has recognized
> that thing as the sign of another thing: a print in the sand indi-
> cates the tiger's passage; a marsh announces a vein of water; the
> hibiscus flower, the end of winter. All the rest is silent and inter-
> changeable; trees and stones are only what they are.
>
> Finally the journey leads to the city of Tamara. You penetrate
> it along streets thick with signboards jutting from the walls. The
> eye does not see things but images of things that mean other
> things: pincers point out the tooth-drawer's house; a tankard, the
> tavern; halberds, the barracks; scales, the grocer's. Statues and
> shields depict lions, dolphins, towers, stars: a sign that some-
> thing—who knows what?—has as its sign a lion or a dolphin or a
> tower or a star. . . . your gaze scans the streets as if they were
> written pages: the city says everything you must think, makes you
> repeat her discourse, and while you believe you are visiting
> Tamara you are only recording the names with which she defines
> herself and all her parts.

Or Eudoxia—

> In Eudoxia, which spreads both upward and down, with winding
> alleys, steps, dead ends, hovels, a carpet is preserved in which you
> can observe the city's true form. . . .
>   An oracle was questioned about the mysterious bond
> between two objects so dissimilar as the carpet and the city. One
> of the two objects—the oracle replied—has the form the gods
> gave the starry sky and the orbits in which the worlds revolve; the
> other is an approximate reflection, like every human creation.
>   For some time the augurs had been sure that the carpet's
> harmonious pattern was of divine origin. The oracle was inter-
> preted in this sense, arousing no controversy. But you could,
> similarly, come to the opposite conclusions: that the true map
> of the universe is the city of Eudoxia, just as it is, a stain that
> spreads out shapelessly, with crooked streets, houses that
> crumble one upon the other amid clouds of dust, fires, screams
> in the darkness.

Marco Polo's récits, like his travels, do not begin or end and are themselves, like the cities, constituted of differences, deferments, apparitions that vanish and return in slightly different forms, traces of sensory stimuli stored in memory, overdetermined symbols of objects seen or imagined, visited or dreamed, hypothesized or depicted on the Protean atlas of Kublai Khan. Minimal shifts in perception underlying his sense of *déjà vu* or his memories have the same value as the largest distance between any two cities in curved space or any two moments in multidimensional time. Repetitions occur often in the narration and in the dialogue of Marco Polo and the Khan, even entire paragraphs. Narration begins in the present, shifts to the past descriptive, ends again in the present ("make them endure, give them space"), uniting time and space even semantically. In fact, time and space are interchangeable and complementary in the metonymic and metaphoric processes of discourse. For both Calvino and Marco Polo they are devices of representation, forms of a plural, decentered subject projecting, repeating, going over and around a self that is as empty as the eye of the tornado. So discourse is continually coiled upon itself and that is why it escapes the chronologic of narrative, destroys narrative rules, actions, characters, negates the organization by coordinates of time and space, no longer follows the pattern of the genre, and therefore succeeds in uncoding or exploding the genre itself.

The filigree design, the tracery of a pattern so subtle it could escape the termites' gnawing, is the form of the imagination whose discourse insinuates itself in the interstices of narrative as the imagination steals into the interstices of the given, which is discrete. For Calvino, the imagination is only imagination of the possible, of potentialities and possibilities not (yet) realized, the unmaking of what is and the making of what could be. *Invisible Cities* is a metaphor, an interpretant of the episteme of our times: there is no presence, no origin, no moment of plenitude, and no absolute form of knowledge; but underneath the continuous labor of the imagination to produce new forms there is a sort of discourse which is not static order reflecting an ordered cosmos, but a complex dynamic interplay of codes and messages. Calvino's universe is a "chaosmos," existing in and because of the ambiguity of signs and their constantly shifting codes.

III

Since I have stated that the three models were not chosen at random, a metacritical discussion of that choice is now necessary. To say that Calvino is familiar with those areas of theoretical speculation, however true and demonstrable the statement may be, is not sufficient, for he certainly is just as familiar with others, as another critic might have pointed out. The models, therefore, are not 1) the only ones applicable to this text or to contemporary narrative, 2) the best or most valuable *in themselves*, or 3) exhaustive or in any way normative. To be sure, they were selected subjectively, as meaning is constructed in the interaction of the reader with the text in a process in which "L'objet dont il est question n'est pas donné: il ne peut être qu'un objet *contsruit* par l'analyste." But if the reader proposes her or his construction as an interpretant which interposes itself between the "tutor" text (to use Barthes's term) and other readers, the subjective becomes public and may, indeed must, be questioned. In his critique of *S/Z*, Fredric Jameson correctly points to the ideological limits of Barthes's notions of textuality and the dangers of an interpretive approach that sees the text, particularly the modernist or postmodern text, as "a triumphant plural, unimpoverished by any constraint of representation [where] the networks are many and interact, without any one of them being about to surpass the rest; this text is a galaxy of signifiers, not a structure of signifieds; it has no beginning; it is reversible; we gain access to it by several entrances, none of which can be authoritatively declared to be the main one." Such "critical pluralism," Jameson notes, "is at best a refusal to go about the principal critical business of our time, which is to forge a kind of methodological synthesis from the multiplicity of critical codes ("The Ideology of the Text"). Though I cannot agree with Jameson's at times uncritical assimilation of semiotic theory and criticism to linguistics-oriented structuralist texual analysis, he is correct in spotting the straw-man argument against representation in the current version of the modernism-realism debate, and the deconstructionists' blindness to their own ideological presuppositions. Unquestionably, the role of ideology in the text is all but clear, particularly in criticism sophisticated enough to acknowledge the dependence of each text on factors of literary tradition and the history of esthetic forms. I think, however, that ideology must be seen both as an informing conceptual system permeating the production, the "pratique signifiante" (Kristeva), of the text, and as a function of the critical process. Thus, rather than merely producing a second, unrelated and entirely personal text in emulation of the one in question, the critic does engage with the text in a two-way critical relationship where subjectivity is not exempt from the obligation of communicative discourse. Unlike Barthes's codes, which are conceived of as being *in* the text itself, the notion of extratextual models brought to bear on the text permits exits from, as well as entrances into, the work. Furthermore, although subjectively chosen, they can be objectively verifed and historically evaluated. The main question is their implicative value, that is, how useful they are in accounting for the formal mechanisms operative in the textual system and in linking those mechanisms to wider sociocultural ones.

The first model I proposed deals with the broad narrative patterns, or what Metz calls "la grande syntagmatique." In the consistent operation of subversion of the most traditional among literary and popular genres that is almost a trademark of Calvino's narrative, it is impossible not to see the intent to undercut the certainties of bourgeois expectations as to the durability of social structures, and the cathartic value of classical plots whose resolution guarantees the inevitability of a presumed "natural" order; but, unlike most avant-garde fiction, Calvino is bent on recuperating the real and positive components of a popular and indigenous tradition displaced by the ruling class for its own purposes of dominance. He is, in other words, very careful not to throw out the baby with the bath water, not to further alienate from their creative sources the real addressees of his message. At a more technical level of formal construction, the second model concerns code innovation. The notion of code, borrowed by literary criticism from linguistics and other areas of communications research, is most often used either in the (linguistic) sense of set of internal rules organizing the elements within one system (i.e., Saussure's *langue*), or in a generalized way to indicate a supposedly homogeneous subset of elements in a complex system. The latter usage applies, for example, to the several codes or "languages" that coexist in the theatre or in cinema; and it is also in this sense that Barthes identifies the five codes of Balzac's novella. In both usages, the term "code" refers to a set of formal rules or elements of content *internal* to the work, and thus emphasizes the signifying aspect of the object studied over its communicative purpose; it focuses the attention on the object in isolation rather than on the process of signification-communication in which the object interacts with the reader/viewer and properly becomes a text. If, on the other hand, a code is defined by Eco as a conventionally (i.e., socially) established correlation between signs and contents, between the elements of a signifying system that make up a message and the meaning attributed to them by the receiver(s) of the message, then messages and codes act upon one another and both functives of the correlation (code) become passible of change; thus a text can contribute to reshaping cultural conventions and consequently our view of the world, of nature, history, even our perception of the physical universe. In fact, Eco further suggests,

> The dialectic between codes and messages, whereby the codes control the emission of messages, but new messages can restructure the codes, constitutes the basis for a discussion on the creativity of language and on its double aspect of "rule-governed creativity" and "rule-changing creativity." (*A Theory of Semiotics*)

In light of this process of semiosis, in which social beings are continually engaged and which affects their lives in a very real way, Calvino's experimentation with iconic and musical modes of textual organization in *Invisible Cities,* or elsewhere with metalanguage or systems other than language such as the tarot or the comic strip, is much more than formalist fun-and-games-in-the-ivory-tower and responds, according to its ability or within the limitations of his craft, to the ideological commitment of expanding and potentiating the human senses.

The third model, relating the mechanisms of textual representation to the psychoanalytic basis of some current theories of the (phenomenological) subject, seems especially useful as a tool of discourse analysis. It is perhaps only in the context of the whole of Calvino's literary and critical writing that his stylistic quest, the search for different modes of distancing (Brecht's *Verfremdungseffekt*) his materials, of posing through the *persona* the antino my subject-object, or investigating the relation of the writer to the subject of writing, can be seen fully. For, if Calvino's stories of human activity and creativity from prehistory to a future imaginable only in science fiction terms, a history with no privileged moments or individuals, point to a nonwestern, antiimperialist, socialist vision, he is also historically aware of being a western man, for whom language and rationality still are the primary vehicles of communication and social organization, and as such must be used, imaginatively and creatively, as a safeguard against ever impending disaster. However meaningless the whole of history might seem to the present excruciating pain of the self, there is no better way to be human than to redirect desire as a social force and to participate in the joint effort of transforming our past into our future.

> Already the Great Khan was leafing through his atlas, over the maps of the cities that menace in nightmares and maledictions: Enoch, Babylon, Yahooland, Butua, Brave New World.
>
> He said: "It is all useless, if the last landing place can only be the infernal city, and it is there that, in ever-narrowing circles, the current is drawing us."
>
> And Polo said: "The inferno of the living is not something that will be; if there is one, it is what is already here, the inferno where we live every day, that we form by being together. There are two ways to escape suffering it. The first is easy for many: accept the inferno and become such a part of it that you can no longer see it. The second is risky and demands constant vigilance and apprehension: seek and learn to recognize who and what, in the midst of the inferno, are not inferno, then make them endure, give them space."

IV

I have offered, so far, three models for Calvino, but a fourth one must be added. Operative diffusely throughout the text, perhaps as the ideological support of the very conditions of representation, there is a hidden process that can be explained only by a dialectical model. All of Calvino's production is characterized by a movement back and forth between the real, the given (narrative genre, dominant cultural assumptions, daily life situations or events) and the possible (new structures of narrativity, unpredictable developments, unexpected forms of life and social organization). At the basis of this dialectic, articulated on the tension between subject and object, is the Marxian notion of alienation. While in his earlier works (notably *The Path to the Nest of Spiders* and "realist" novellas like *Smog* or *The Watcher*) he was concerned with the representation of alienation in concrete historical, social, and emotional conditions, though never reducing the human person to an emblem or society to a statistical abstraction. In his more recent works his concern is esthetic representation itself and what might be called the literary displacement of the relation of alienation.

In the complex evolution of social history, further complicated by the uneven development of socioeconomic and artistic forms, the militant artist is always caught between love and belief in art as one of the highest forms of human creativity, and the well-founded fear that art is impotent to change the world. The dilemma is real but insoluble if posited in these terms. If social reality is too complex and multilevelled, too much unlike a surface that may be reflected in a mirror, art can only be indirect, mediated representation of the most important aspects of a given historical moment of society. Perhaps all that should be asked of art is that it succeed in expressing the potential and the will to change, not just by transposing symbolically the present or past conditions, but by constructing, out of those, imaginary diagrams of possiblities in the future, leaving to the whole of society (of which the artist is only one member, equal to the others) the task of their realization. From this viewpoint, Calvino's work is not only an epistemological metaphor but a diagram for praxis, a model that has its place side by side with the models I have proposed as its interpretants. His conviction that the collectively created folk tales provided to the feudal peasant society "a general explanation of life . . . the catalogue of destinies possible to a man or a woman," a system of values and parameters of behavior, carries over to his own modern tales. In *Invisible Cities* the overall frame of the dialogue between the doubles, Marco Polo and Kublai Khan, dramatizes the dialectic tension in contemporary society between alienation (*Entfremdung*) and conscious objectification (*Vergegenständlichung*). Kublai Khan, the Hegelian ruler, attempts to control or possess his incomprehensible, ungovernable, decaying empire by reducing it to a game of chess played in the sphere of mind, ultimately to negate its very existence. Marco Polo, the traveller, the exchanger, the trader of symbols, constantly reaffirms the world's physical and social existence as a result of human desire, labor, and production.

"The emperor is he who is a foreigner to each of his subjects, and only through foreign eyes and ears could the empire manifest its existence to Kublai." As Marco Polo, at first ignorant of the Tartars' language, mimes for the emperor the wonders he has seen, "in the Khan's mind the empire was reflected in a desert of labile and interchangeable data. . . . Perhaps, Kublai thought, the empire is nothing but a Zodiac of the mind's phantasms. 'On the day when I know all the emblems,' he asked Marco, 'shall I be able to possess my empire at last?' And the Venetian answered: 'Sire, do not believe it. On that day you will be an emblem among emblems.'" The emperor keeps sending Marco to distant lands in the hope that the traveller's accounts will give him knowledge and control of his empire. Once, upon his return, Marco is asked to describe the cities he has visited by means of huge chess pieces of polished ivory. Devoured by the need to possess/comprehend reality from his luxurious palace, the Khan resorts to ever increasing abstraction and keeps Marco playing endless games of chess.

Knowledge of the empire was hidden in the pattern drawn by the angular shifts of the knight, by the diagonal passages opened by the bishop's incursions, by the lumbering, cautious tread of the king and the humble pawn, by the inexorable ups and downs of every game.

The Great Khan tried to concentrate on the game: but now it was the game's purpose that eluded him. Each game ends in a gain or a loss: but of what? . . . By disembodying his conquests to reduce them to the essential, Kublai had arrived at the extreme operation: the definitive conquest, of which the empire's multiform treasures were only illusory envelopes. It was reduced to a square of planed wood: nothingness.

In the next dialogue section, eight pages and five cities later, this last paragraph is repeated verbatim, not only to signify the continuous flow of thought in the dialectic subject, but also to reascertain the thesis of which Marco's response constitutes the dialectic opposite, the antithesis.

Then Marco Polo spoke: "your chessboard, sire, is inlaid with two woods: ebony and maple. The square on which your enlightened gaze is fixed was cut from the ring of a trunk that grew in a year of drought: you see how its fibers are arranged? . . ." The quantity of things that could be read in a little piece of smooth and empty wood overwhelmed Kublai; Polo was already talking about ebony forests, about rafts laden with logs that come down the rivers, of docks, of women at the windows.

An emperor is an emperor is an emperor, and a traveller is a traveller is a traveller. The context of the problematics is again the opposition of mind to nature; of abstract, depersonalized knowledge to sensuous, creative participation; of dominance and alienation to productive objectification as positive and joyous human act. In this perspective, Calvino's choice of "characters" for his unorthodox narrative takes on a significance that goes well beyond the mythical resonance of the adventures of the first popular culture hero of the west (for Odysseus is a classical hero and like Greek or Roman mythology he has always belonged to the ruling social classes since the Renaissance, never becoming a part of the Christian popular traditions established in Europe in the Middle Ages). Marco Polo, the ancestor of Columbus and of today's space travellers, is the symbol of a rising, progressive, open-frontier society on its way to building, through trade and exchange, one of the most prosperous and sophisticated civilizations in the world. In contrast with the previous Roman and Arab empires in the Mediterranean area, based like the "Tartar Empire" on military conquest and dominance of their subjects, Marco Polo symbolizes the new pre-Renaissance vision of a world in which people interact with one another peacefully and constructively by exchanging goods and physical and intellectual resources (who doesn't know that Marco Polo brought from the Orient not only gunpowder and the silk-worm, but noodles as well?).

Yet Calvino has not written a historical novel, and all these considerations remain implicit in the broad connotative frame of his work. It is not our past history that *Invisible Cities* represents, or even developments from current history: looking at the Khan's atlas Marco Polo imagines a city "which might be called San Francisco . . . and which might blossom as capital of the Pacific a millennium hence, after the long siege of three hundred years that would lead the races of the yellow and the black and the red to fuse with the surviving descendants of the whites in an empire more vast than the Great Khan's." We know, as Calvino does, that the visions and aspirations of the early mercantile society of Marco Polo were superseded and negated by the reified and alienated society of capitalism already latent within it. If Marco Polo represents the positive, creative forces and Kublai Khan symbolizes their antithesis, the moment of negativity, their dialogue, in which Marco succeeds in having the last word (but only until the next chapter, or the next command by the Khan), is a dynamic model for the dialectics of history. By opting not to present Marco Polo in his real historical context and by making him exchange parables, images, and signs rather than objects, Calvino stresses the semiosic nature of sociocultural reality, that is to say that the meanings attributed to objects and relations, rather than the objects themselves, constitute human reality. If those meanings exist by virtue of social conventions of perception, representation, conceptualization, then the change in social reality both effects and is effected by the transformation of existing conventions or codes. I suggested earlier that *Invisible Cities* is an epistemological metaphor and a model for praxis in the sense that it represents possible ways of knowing, perceiving, coding experience and reality. In Calvino's model, alienation is the constitutive moment of the contemporary human condition symbolized in the fragmented and dialectic subject Marco Polo-Kublai Khan. But insofar as the semiosic activity can transform the given, alienation can be overcome, if only temporarily, in the ongoing, open-ended historical process, by human creativity.

The continuing chain or open series of the cities, reflected *en abîme* within each city, corresponds to the production of objects and signs, subsequent reification and alienation, and negation of the alienation by a transformation which is itself a new production. An exact, and deeply moving, representation of this process, which in Calvino's personal thematics is always connected with desire as the moving force of human history, where the personal and the political are inextricably intertwined, can be found in the city of Zobeide,

> the white city, well exposed to the moon, with streets wound about themselves as in a skein. They tell this tale of its foundation: men of various nations had an identical dream. They saw a woman running at night through an unknown city; she was seen from behind, with long hair, and she was naked. They dreamed of pursuing her. As they twisted and turned, each of them lost her. After the dream they set out in search of that city; they never found it, but they found one another; they decided to build a city like the one in the dream. In laying out the streets, each followed the course of his pursuit; at the spot where they had lost the fugitive's trail, they arranged spaces and walls differently from the dream, so she would be unable to escape again.
>
> This was the city of Zobeide, where they settled, waiting for that scene to be repeated one night. None of them, asleep or awake, ever saw the woman again. The city's streets were streets where they went to work every day, with no link any more to the dreamed chase. Which, for that matter, had long been forgotten.
>
> New men arrived from other lands, having had a dream like theirs, and in the city of Zobeide, they recognized something of the streets of the dream, and they changed the positions of arcades and stairways to resemble more closely the path of the pursued woman and so, at the spot where she had vanished, there would remain no avenue of escape.
>
> Those who had arrived first could not understand what drew these people to Zobeide, this ugly city, this trap.

That the parable ends with the negative moment, "ugly" and "trap" being contemporary signifiers of alienation and reification, is a measure of Calvino's moral consistency. The demonstratives "these" and "this," presentifying the perception through the first group's free indirect discourse, are a small but subtle example of his stylistic mastery: the text is left open, a representation at once of social process and of itself as creative process.

OLGA RAGUSA

Italo Calvino:
The Repeated Conquest of Contemporaneity

"With all the variety and innovation of your writing, how would you define your work as a whole? What would you see as the ultimate purpose of your writing?"

"I write each book as though it were the first I've ever written—as if it had no relation whatever to any of the others. I'd leave the task of defining my work to the critic."
—Italo Calvino, in Markeq, "The Contemporary Fabulist" [interview].

Like Pirandello, Italo Calvino has repreatedly insisted that his works originate in images and not in ideas. Both writers have wanted to shake off the straitjacket of philosophical and theoretical abstractions that critics—true to their vocation of intellectualizing art—have too often forced on them. Pirandello's expression of intolerance derives from an almost physical malaise, the fear of being imprisoned or limited; it is a cry for freedom, a passionate denunciation of the evil men do to one another. Calvino's statements are matter-of-fact, informative, not polemical. In speaking about his differences with a fellow writer, Carlo Cassola, he is amusingly self-revealing when he says that both of them in the course of a discussion tend to render their positions extreme: "I become more and more obstinate especially to get him

From *World Literature Today* 57, no. 2 (Spring 1983). © 1983 *World Literature Today*.

angry and also a little because I believe in what I'm saying; he becomes even more obstinate because he believes in what he is saying and a little also to get me angry" (my translations of Calvino's works throughout). The contrast in attitudes between him and Cassola, the comparative dosage of belief and provocation, emphasizes Calvino's capacity for remaining cool, ironically detached, inclined to laugh where another person might burn with righteous indignation or become withdrawn in resigned melancholy. Calvino's joie de vivre—or *joie d'écrire*—in spite of disenchantment, his basic acceptance of things as they are without being blind to their insufficiencies, his ability to make the best of the ceaseless activity of modern life, to recharge his energy from the same sources that feed changes in industry, international relations, dominant ideologies, literary criticism, journalism and art—all these mark him as in tune with the contemporary world.

To a greater degree than most writers of fiction, perhaps, Calvino has been generous with a wide range of published comments on his works. They are often retrospective, accompanying a new edition of a work, but they may also be contemporaneous with the work or even precede it. What distinguishes these writings is their direct confrontation with specific works and with the author's career as a writer. They are elaborate curricula vitae, presentations of work done or to be done, sophisticated blurbs, press releases—the unavoidable frame that modern mass communication and the rapid turnover in the production of the printed word demand and require. In comparison to the large quantity of material which could be subsumed under the rubric of "Calvino on Calvino"—and which makes the critic's work almost redundant—Pirandello's not infrequent comments on his writings shrink to near-insignificance. But in the one instance as in the other, whatever the impression at first sight, it would be improper to speak of self-promotion. Pirandello's rage to be heard, his vindication of man's right to assert his individuality, to speak his "reason," is paralleled by Calvino's impersonal chronicling of his literary and intellectual trajectory, by his factual, unemotional recounting of his professional activities. If the image of the romantic poet still hovers in the background of Pirandello's bourgeois persona, it has been completely replaced in Calvino's case by the gray suit of the businessman or the more informal turtleneck sweater of the professional intellectual (the *operatore culturale*, to use a recent expression). In this respect too Calvino is unmistakably contemporary.

In terms of literary career as measured by a writer's continued active presence on the literary scene, Calvino's has from the outset been a success story. The ebullient affirmation of storytelling which marked his debut as a writer immediately following the end of World War II reverberates in the apparent ease with which he has been able to renew himself for almost forty years now. Calvino's success is no literary "case." It is an extraordinarily fortunate beginning followed by continuing growth in an accretion and transformation of meanings won not by retreat from the surrounding world but by acceptance of its riches and contrasts, by exploiting it "to turn facts into words," constructing not "a duplicate copy of life" but an equivalent to it. Calvino is neither a realist painter or photographer nor yet a poet turned storyteller; it is neither the world outside he wishes to capture and hold, nor the evanescence of his own states of consciousness, his inner self, that he is anxious to explore and express. He finds that the cinema and the press have successfully and definitively taken over the "task of the minute representation of their time which was the burden and the glory of literature in the nineteenth century." And he has stated bluntly that he is not interested in "psychology, spiritual life, interiors, the family, customs, society." When he is not telling stories, he functions as an intellectual, sometimes as a scholar: up-to-date on new works and ideas, in touch with what is being thought, written and read, engaged in the life of the mind not as introspection and meditation but as activity, productivity and performance.

More important in this respect than his formal education (he has a degree in English from the University of Turin, earned with a dissertation on Conrad) were his years of editorial work for the publisher Einaudi, which date from the publication of his first book, *Il sentiero dei nidi di ragno* (1947; translated as *The Path of the Nest of Spiders*, 1957), and his militant journalism, first in the pages of the Communist daily *L'Unità* and later, between 1959 and 1966, as co-director with Elio Vittorini of the journal *Il Menabò*. Indicative of the coherence of his literary career is the fact that virtually all his books have been published by Einaudi in handsomely produced and for the most part inexpensive editions, distinguished by illustrated covers which propose visual equivalents to the text in vignettes taken from the minimal art of a Paul Klee or a Saul Steinberg. It is customary to present the significance of the Einaudi imprint almost exclusively in terms of the writers and intellectuals who have gathered around the publishing house: Pavese and Vittorini, Natalia Ginzburg and Carlo Levi. But it is well to remember that Einaudi differs from other major Italian publishers not only in editorial policy, which determines the selection of titles (including translations) for publication, but also in the commitment to its writers, measured by its willingness to keep the backlist in print. To a greater degree than other commercial publishers Einaudi has interpreted its main function as that of serving Italian culture: first under Fascism by ensuring that the lines of communication with intellectual life outside Italy remained open, and later in the early post–World War II years by the massive introduction into Italy of works that had been excluded for political and ideological reasons during the preceding twenty years—Marx, Brecht, Lukács, Adorno, Aragon, Auerbach, Gramsci, Jung and Benjamin, among others. At Einaudi, then, Calvino found himself in a stimulating and formative environment, more an intellectual training ground than a moneymaking enterprise.

As alluded to earlier, Calvino's literary production has almost from the beginning been accompanied by critical efforts to track its evolution. His precocious success (he was barely twenty-four when *Il sentiero dei nidi di ragno* was published) attracted more than the ordinary share of attention to each of his subsequent works. It came as a surprise when in 1952 he left his neorealist beginnings to veer full course into the realm of fantasy. In the novel and in the short stories collected in *Ultimo viene il corvo* (1949; *Adam, One Afternoon and Other Stories*, 1957), the setting had been the Resistance, more precisely Partisan warfare in the mountainous terrain that presses upon the Ligurian shore of Genoa and San Remo (the latter the old European vacation paradise where Calvino grew up). The characters had been persons, recognizable individuals, involved in human situations and contemporary dilemmas. They may not have been presented with the full genealogy, personal history and psychological assessment of figures in nineteenth-century novels but instead with shorthand notations such as are used in drama or in the short narrative genres; still, they were not for that any the less "real." Their names were most frequently nicknames and epithets (Pin, il Dritto, Mancino, Maria la Matta), their features and gait sketched with a few strokes, their speech monosyllabic, full of expletives, colloquial. They had almost no revealed inner life. But these were familiar narrative procedures: the lack of depth in portrayal, of written density on the page, were part and parcel of the thinning out, the stripping down that the novel had begun to undergo even before neorealism.

As for the sentiments expressed in Calvino's early work, the positions taken, the ethical judgments made, the distinctions between right and wrong, good and bad, however superficial and unnuanced they actually were—the pronouncements of youth after all, no more than so many "givens"—they sounded right, and eventually he and others like him in the mainstream of postwar European literature ended up by imposing their view of recent history in creating the not yet exploded myth of the Resistance. In 1964, when Calvino wrote a preface to a new edition of *Il sentiero dei nidi di ragno*, he was still able to recapture effortlessly the euphoria of those years, the sense of a new beginning, of the "defiant gaiety" with which his generation faced the future, and the veritable explosion of storytelling that appeared to unite a whole people in the recounting of a common experience: "In the trains that were beginning to run again, crowded with people and sacks of flour and oil cans, every passenger was telling his neighbors what had happened to him, and the same was true of every customer in the workers' canteens, and of every woman queued at a store. The grayness of everyday life seemed a thing of the past. We moved in the multicolored universe of storytelling." In the years that followed, one might say, it has been Calvino's self-imposed task to re-create the fullness of this initial period, and it has been his fortune to be successful each time in remounting the incline of diminishing creative energy, a hazard in the individual's life in general and an earmark—in the opinion of some at least—of our own troubled times.

The novel Calvino published in 1952, *Il visconte dimezzato* (*The Cloven Viscount*, 1962), turned its back not only on neorealism but even on verisimilitude. Set in the late seventeenth century during the Austro-Turkish Wars, it tells the unlikely story of a knight whose adventures continue even after he is cut in half by a cannonball. In 1957 it was joined by another piece of apparent escapism, *Il barone rampante* (*The Baron in the Trees*, 1957), whose protagonist as a boy of twelve, on 15 June 1767, leaves the family dinner table to climb up an oak tree in the garden and thereby begin a stubborn, uninterrupted arboreal life that will come to an end only with his death a half-century later. Finally, in *Il cavaliere inesistente* (1959; *The Non-Existent Knight*, 1962), Calvino dipped into the chivalric epic and invented a new paladin for Charlemagne, the warrior Agilulfo, who is an empty suit of shining armor, a being all spirit and will and entirely without body. Actually Calvino had thought of *Il visconte dimezzato* as no more than a "divertimento," and had he been able to impose that status on all three works (by publishing them in a periodical, for instance, as he had intended to do with *Il visconte*, or by turning them into children's books, as he did with *Il barone* in 1959 and *Il visconte* in 1975), he might have avoided the need to defend himself against the accusation of disengagement, of having rejected the literature of social consciousness for works of frivolous entertainment. His apologia is contained in the preface to *I nostri antenati* (*Our Ancestors;* 1960), the book that brought together the three novels as a trilogy and thus made them even more visible as turning points. It is a typical exposé of the latent ideological implications of a work of art: what Calvino says in essence is that because external circumstances had changed, he was no longer able to find the right tone for his old subject matter, but that, contrary to what it might seem, the new subject matter was by no means divorced from surrounding reality. Rearranging the three works to respect not the chronology of their composition but the chronology of the historical epochs in which they are set, Calvino was able to privilege the "message" of *Il barone rampante*. The argument runs like this: if in *Il cavaliere* the human experience depicted is that of the conquest of being and in *Il visconte* it is the aspiration to wholeness in spite of the mutilations imposed by society, then *Il barone* charts the

way to an integrity that is not individualistic but is achieved through loyalty
to personal self-determination.

So much for the ideological debate and the relation of Calvino's works of
fantasy to it. But the preface to *I nostri antenati* and a number of essays that
belong to the period of the trilogy reveal more than this. They show Calvino
to be conversant with the dominant trends in the study of literature and with
the various "approaches" to the discussion of the work of art. If his concern
with the relationship between literature and society betrays the leftist foun-
dation of his intellectual orientation (he had resigned from the Communist
Party in 1957), his dissection of the writer's craft, his ability to analyze his
own and others' works as artifacts, as constructed forms, points to his having
been in close contact with twentieth-century developments in the novel in
Italy and the rest of Europe and with the various theories, historical and
structural, that had been advanced to explicate them. He presents the trilogy
on the one hand as a sequence of didactic models for self-realization, "three
steps in the approach to freedom," part of the intellectual's program for
influencing historical processes; but on the other hand he cannot let go of
critical topoi such as narrative voice, identification of author and character,
relationship between theme and plot, the fruition of the work of art in the act
of reading and, finally, the self-conscious focusing on writing itself, on "the
connection between the complexity of life and the sheet of paper on which
this complexity comes to rest in the shape of alphabetical signs."

A great leap forward in Calvino's appropriation of new subject matter,
the next step in his constant *aggiornarsi* or repeated conquest of contemporaneity, comes with *Le cosmicomiche* (1965; *Cosmicomics*, 1968) and *Ti con zero*
(1967; *t Zero*, 1969). In these works, according to some critics, Calvino has
abandoned the anthropocentric view of the universe. And indeed, they mark
a kind of final acceptance—in all its consequences—of the Copernican revolution, an inversion in values that Mattia Pascal (and with him Pirandello)
had still considered a disaster for mankind but that Calvino is able to domi-
nate with a buoyancy reminiscent of the apparent ease with which space
exploration succeeded in finally putting man on the moon. The narrator of
the stories, sketches, vignettes or (to use the term favored by the structural-
ists) "microtexts" that constitute *Le cosmicomiche*, and of two of the segments
into which *Ti con zero* is divided, is a certain Qfvfq, a sentient, conscious
being, sometimes a lowly organism floating in undifferentiated matter, sometimes a New York corporation executive caught in a traffic jam; through him
the evolution of the universe, as it happened or might have happened, is
recounted. Each "chapter" is introduced by a passage of scientific expostion
such as might occur in one of the encyclopedia entries or works of popular-

ization that Calvino refers to as having furnished the images out of which these stories grew, an imaginary space atlas, the modern counterpart to the geographical maps that gave impetus to stories of exploration in other centuries.

The successive conditions of the universe and the theories that account for them are the background for fictional episodes which dramatize and communicate the feeling of such temporally and spatially distant experiences for us as cataclysmic explosions, slow changes in the atmosphere and in the pull of gravitation, the passing of geological eras and periods, the extinction of species, the ever-recurrent alternation of assimilation and differentiation, the attractions and repulsions between like and unlike beings who often have only a residue of the human in them. "How could we get along with one another?" Qfvfq asks at a certain point apropos the clash in reactions between himself, now a New Jersey commuter, and Vug, his old girl friend, rediscovered in front of a Tiffany show window.

> For me only what has homogeneous growth, indistinctness, achieved repose has any value; for her what is disjoined or commingled, either one or the other, or preferably both together. . . . I imagined a slow, uniform expansion like that of crystals, until the "I"-crystal would become interpenetrated with the "she"-crystal and perhaps together we would become one with the world-crystal; she already seemed to know that the law of living matter would be to separate and to come together again endlessly.

Thus the familiar everyday causes of conflict between individuals, the recurrent strains in a marriage, the incompatibilities that exist because of different temperaments and different growth and maturation rates are here expressed with concepts derived not from psychology or sociology, as often in modern fiction, but from physics and chemistry, reminding one that Calvino's family background and his earliest education were in fact dominated by the natural rather than the human sciences.

Like poets who try their hand at translating the poetry of others, Calvino has not only told his own stories, but he has also retold the stories of others. His most important retelling no doubt occurred in *Fiabe italiane* (1956; *Italian Folktales*, 1980), an Einaudi project that kept him occupied between 1954 and 1956. Fiabe italiane was first published in the series "I Millenni," a deluxe collection of world classics begun in 1947 that already included the Brothers Grimm's *Le fiabe del focolare* (1951) and a volume of *Fiabe africane* (1955), for which Calvino had written the preface. In 1957 a volume of *Fiabe francesi*, French folktales of the seventeenth and eighteenth centuries, joined these. Calvino's task included collecting folktales in the various dialects of Italy and translating them into Italian, thus putting together a corpus that could take its place beside the most famous such European collection, the German one. *Fiabe italiane*, which won recognition for its impeccable scholarship, brought Calvino into direct contact with the fund of (as he was himself to write) "the ever repeated and ever varied case histories of human vicissitudes . . . the catalogue of the possible destinies of a man or a woman . . . the drastic division of the living into kings and beggars; the persecution of the innocent . . . the common fate of succumbing to enchantments . . . and the effort to free oneself . . . loyalty to commitments . . . beauty as a sign of grace . . . and especially the unitary substance of all—men, beasts, plants, objects—the infinite possibility of metamorphosis in everything that exists."

Orlando furioso di Ludovico Ariosto raccontato da Italo Calvino (1970) is a different kind of retelling. The work is patterned on those abridged versions of classics in which selected passages are connected by brief summaries of the intervening material. Ariosto's *ottave*, his eight-line stanzas, mingle with Calvino's prose in a reworking that both maintains and varies the structure of the original and emphasizes the reality of the poem as construct, as text. "At the beginning there is only a maiden who flees through the forest. . . . She is the protagonist of a poem that was left unfinished, and she is running to enter another poem barely begun"—thus Calvino begins his retelling, "translating" the recent critical discovery of literariness to indicate the *Furioso*'s link with the *Innamorato* and clearing the hurdle of historical, biographical and cultural contexts. The latter are dealt with in his "Presentation," which, as is usual in introductions to the *Furioso*, starts out with a review of the development of the Charlemagne cycle and continues with a brief sketch of Ariosto's life, culminating with the main themes of the poem and its form. (The indispensable notes, borrowed from Caretti's 1966 edition of *Orlando furioso*, are relegated to an appendix and round out the scholarly apparatus.) Calvino's perceptions of Ariosto's storytelling techniques interest us in particular for what they tell us about his own craft. Three points that he makes are especially worth noting: Ariosto added episodes to the *Innamorato* that spread out in all directions, "intersecting with one another and dividing up to create new symmetries and new contrasts"; the masterly heaping of *ottava* on *ottava* deflects attention from Ariosto himself, keeping him—"this crystal clear, cheerful poet, apparently without a care in the world"—hidden and mysterious; and finally, in the last canto, the poem ends in the presence of its own audience, welcomed by the ladies and gentlemen of the time of its telling, for whom it was composed, and by all those others, "readers present and future who will take part in its game, recognizing themselves in it."

The next two major works are probably Calvino's most difficult ones yet published: *Le città invisibili* (1972; *Invisible Cities*, 1974) and *Il castello dei destini incrociati* (1973; *The Castle of Crossed Destinies*, 1977). Both are related to his retelling of the stories of others and to the structural analyses of story-telling which accompanied and grew out of the emergence of the nouveau roman. They have a programmatic, mediated origin; they are intentional more than spontaneous. In the postcript to *Il castello* Calvino himself has told about the double genesis of this work: a 1968 international seminar at which one of the contributors dealt with fortune-telling and the language of emblems; and the decision of the publisher Franco Maria Ricci to bring out an art book on the Visconti tarot cards preserved by museums in Bergamo and New York. When the assignment from the publisher came, Calvino had already been at work on another deck of tarots, the so-called Marseilles deck, which provided the visual stimuli for "La taverna dei destini incrociati" (The Tavern of Crossed Destinies), the second text of the completed work. Obviously the operative concept is that of "crossed destinies" rather than that of "castle" as opposed to "tavern" as cultural and sociological referents; this is corroborated by the fact that Calvino at one point planned a third text, "Il motel dei destini incrociati," built on vignettes from comic strips, which he describes as "the contemporary equivalent of the tarot cards as a representation of the collective unconscious." Calvino's project was to let the cards tell the story, as in divination, bearing in mind that any single card has no inherent meaning, only one derived from its place in a sequence, and that at the end of the game all the cards must have been used. Reversing the usual order, instead of looking for pictorial illustrations for a text already written—as had been the case, for instance, in the "I Millenni" edition of the *Fiabe*—the starting point here is a picture, a sign with many meanings. The self-imposed rules, the many determinants, turned the assignment into a nightmare, a maddening puzzle, a placing and replacing of cards that was cut short only by publication.

The frame for both sets of stories in *Il castello* is embedded in a device of the fabulatory tradition of the West which goes back to the *Decameron* and the *Canterbury Tales* and which was still very much alive on the reduced scale of the single story in the flowering of short fiction in the nineteenth century. A group of travelers gathers about a table, and soon, as on the Italian trains after the war recalled earlier, they are deep in the exchange of tales. But the lightheartedness of that now distant experience is lacking in *Il castello*, whose special twist is that the travelers on their way through the forest—locus of the folktale but also of the *Divine Comedy* and of many of the episodes of the *Furioso*—have lost their speech because of their horrible and fearful encounters. It is true that on the table—in one case richly set and lit by chandeliers, in the other strewn with rough bowls and mugs, the gloom barely dissipated by a smoky candle—each group finds a pack of cards through which to communicate. But the communication is difficult, and though the suspense generated by the successive emergence of cards is sufficient to keep the travelers alert, the reader must be endowed with an uncommon literary education to appreciate Calvino's sleights of hand—the evoking of Faust and Macbeth, Oedipus and Parsifal, Hamlet and Orlando. Thus this work has been received most enthusistically by academic critics, whose intellectual pleasure in unraveling tight constructions may distort the total effect of this slim volume. The effect, for me at least, is not unlike that of "Il conte di Montecristo" (the last story in *Ti con zero*). In that retelling Calvino had emphasized the efforts of Edmond Dantès and of the Abbé Faria to escape from the Castle of If, relating them emblematically to the manner in which Dumas *père* and his assistants had put the novel together. Perhaps because the subject is the blocked liberation from an impregnable fortress, from an oppressive concentration-camplike environment, the proliferation of hypothetically possible but actually impossible escape routes and the repeated production and elimination of alternative developments in Dumas's compositional strategy are not accompanied by the usual ebullience, the youthful, life-affirming joyfulness we are accustomed to find in Calvino's coming to grips with diversity and open-endedness.

No such impediment to full enjoyment exists in *Le città invisibili* and in *Se una notte d'inverno un viaggiatore* (1979; *If on a Winter's Night a Traveler*, 1981). In the first work the brilliant writing and the optimistic "message" redeem the burden of an intellectual structure which plays with variations on the organizing themes modestly announced in the chapter headings. These imaginary Eastern cities, suggested by that mercantile version of *The Thousand and One Nights*, Marco Polo's *Il milione*, have released an unsuspected richness of incantatory words, and the moral lesson—that one must learn to live in the midst of evil by recognizing the little that is not evil and making room for it to flourish—is sufficiently understated to appeal to a generation of readers suspicious of high-sounding promises and radical panaceas. In the second work, *Se una notte d'inverno un viaggiatore*, frame story and framed stories are finally, triumphantly integrated. The frame story is about nothing less than "ce vice impuni, la lecture," and in the early chapters we get an almost complete phenomenology of the book as artifact and text such as only someone who has been personally involved with all aspects of book production could so effortlessly provide. The framed stories are actually only beginnings of stories, interrupted novels, tantalizing way stations on the road that leads the Reader and that other reader, Ludmilla his beloved, to the large double bed where each is last seen reading his/her book. And thus, we may presume, they lived happily ever after.

It might be asked in conclusion: What are the chances of survival for an oeuvre so embedded in contemporaneity, so consequent in its denial of the weight and conditioning of the past, so successful in achieving freshness and novelty for its every new component? Calvino was admired from the start, and he now has a public that circles the globe. At the very time when the printed word is on so many sides beleaguered by other media, he has conquered the readers that count by taking them into his confidence, by showing them not the world, but the world of the writer. May the critic, the other kind of reader, that subversive spoilsport, deal light-handedly with that world, guarding it against destruction.

LINDA C. BADLEY

Calvino engagé: *Reading as Resistance in* If on a Winter's Night a Traveler

Italo Calvino's first novel, *The Path to the Nest of Spiders* (1947), came out of his formative experience in the anti-fascist resistance. According to some critics, his fiction has subsequently alienated itself: in the fifties, in the fractured fairy tales of the trilogy *I nostri antenati;* in the sixties, in the science-fiction fantasy of *Cosmicomics* and *t zero;* in the seventies, in the surface play of metafiction. John Barth may have sealed his reputation in America in "The Literature of Replenishment" (1980), an essay which in effect damns him as an exemplary postmodernist.

Perhaps this reputation is deserved. Calvino's next-to-last novel, *The Castle of Crossed Destinies* (1973), has in particular come under attack for its theoretical pretensions. A permutated sequence of card tricks, it invites one to examine *ad infinitum* its structualist subtext. In a concluding note, Calvino admits to publishing it "to be free of" the "diabolical idea of conjuring up all the stories that could be contained in a tarot deck," a mania that began as early as his exhaustive compilation of *Italian Folktales* in 1956. His latest book, *If on a Winter's Night a Traveler* (1979), betrays a similar "rage for order"—so much that, in the words of Melvin Maddocks, "anything seems possible except that Calvino, 57, now an editor of the Turin house Giulio Einaudi Editore, was once a Marxist, a veteran of World War II resistance, who believed, in his youth, that literature should be dedicated

From *Perspectives in Contemporary Literature* (1984). © 1984 by *Perspectives in Contemporary Literature*.

to 'political engagement,' to 'social battle'("Mirror Writing" in *Time*).

In several respects Calvino's last book is his most bookish. As metafiction it resembles the episode in which Thurber, after observing plant cells under a microscope, presents his botany instructor with a drawing of his own eye. Overtly recalling the mazes of Borges or Nabokov, Calvino's novel is an editor's nightmare in whose atmosphere the ghost of Roland Barthes hovers. The frame story takes the reader on a wild goose chase, a search for the true text of *If on a Winter's Night a Traveler*, lost through an error in binding, the signature having been repeated throughout the volume in what becomes an infinite regression. The hero, an unnamed male reader, returns to the bookstore to find that Calvino's book has been mixed with a Polish novel he has unknowingly been reading. Choosing to finish that one, he finds himself in yet another country—the style is sharp, unfamiliar, the names are not Polish, and so on. Through such mystifying permutations, Calvino telescopes ten books from around the world into one and so creates the Barthesian world as text—or a surreal picture of his day-to-day grind, of bringing order out of the prolix chaos of "pages, lines, words, whirling in a dust storm" ⟨translation by William Weaver throughout⟩.

Calvino's plot is engaged, to be sure, with politics—with terrorist organizations, conspiracies, censors, and the like—all militating against the writer. Its concern is really, as in John Barth's conspiracy-ridden *Letters* (1979), the politics of print. The plot is generated by a plot attributed to the translator Ermes Marana, founder of OEPHLW (Organization for the Electronic Production of Homogenized Literary Works), to "flood the world" with a "literature of apocrypha, of false attributions, of imitations and counterfeits and pastiches." Marana, representing the mass media (his head is "oblong horizontally, like a dirigible," has paralyzed best-selling author Silas Flannery, upon whose creativity the world's economy depends. The "numerous novels" for which he has received advances involve "financing on an international level"; the "liquor to be drunk by the characters," the "furnishings, gadgets," and so forth, all of which are under contract, "remain unfinished, at the mercy of his spiritual crisis." World peace depends on his (or Marana's) ability to supply an insatiable Persian Gulf Sultana with the novels required in her marriage contract. As in the frame tale of the Arabian Nights, a major source of Calvino's inspiration, the fate of civilization hangs on the word, the ability of Flannery, a fan of Snoopy, to get beyond "It was a dark and stormy night. . . ." Residing in Alpine alienation (and recalling Joyce and Nabokov), Flannery does nothing but write in a diary and observe through a telescope a young woman in a deck chair in a valley who is reading a book—is it his? Eventually it is, like all the books within the book, *If on a Winter's Night a Traveler*, by "Italo Calvino," who like Flannery and the real

Calvino has not published a novel in several years. As Flannery muses, "Perhaps the true book is this diary in which I try to note down the image of the woman in the deck chair at the various hours of the day, as I observe her in the changing light."

Indirectly conspiring against the Author is the radical structuralist-feminist Critic, Lotaria, whose computer-assisted thesis decodes Flannery's words as fast as he can write them. Inevitably she presses the wrong key and erases an original, leaving it "crumpled, dissolved, . . . like a sand dune blown away by the wind." Militating from the right are firms pressuring Flannery with schemes to complete his novels mechanically. "[T]his is the moment," we are told "when self-realization on paper is sought not so much by isolated individuals as by collectives."

The collectives and conspiracies have one thing in common. They are external manifestations of the impulse to order taken to an extreme in mechanization and replication, which regresses to disorder and entropy. What modernist Wallace Stevens called the "Blessed rage for order" is now ecologically and politically unsound, resulting in the sort of cosmic scrawl—the "general thickness of signs superimposed and coagulated"—that subsumes the universe at the end of *Cosmicomics*' "A Sign in Space." The problem is inherent in the individual act of writing, as Calvino pointed out as early as "Smog" (1958), a story from his neorealistic period about a Marxist journalist employed by an anti-pollution journal owned by the pollutors. For the postmodernist Calvino, it seems, the "fascist machine" or enemy to be resisted is inherent in the medium; the world war is the media blitz, to be fought by the individual against himself—against his invariable but perverse attraction to the mechanical, the "diabolical" temptation (in Calvino's case) to turn the tarot deck into a "machine for constructing stories." It is from this perspective that Calvino has for some time been *engagé.*

The full title of *If on a Winter's Night* strings together those of the pseudo-novels, all of which are in some sense attributable to Marana's forging enterprises. Thus Calvino exposes his complicity with the perpetrators of a literature of "bad faith," exposing the paradox of the author's position, that in the act of writing he contributes to the collective scrawl. Not Marana, Lotaria, or even surrogate author Flannery, but Calvino must be held ultimately responsible for this mess. All four writers, moreover, are ordering reality for the same purpose: not for power or money but for the muse—the attention of the mysterious woman in the deck chair who is always absorbed in her book and so, however passively and paradoxically, resisting.

Such paradoxes are hardly original, having informed for some time the self-reflexive pages of Nabokov, Borges, and Barth. The "literature of exhaustion," as Barth calls it, by definition puts up a poor resistance. What

Fredric Jameson says of structuralist criticism applies here: signifying nothing other than itself as language or form, it imprisons itself in its terms, to which it loops back in infinite regress. Or like Calvino's Professor Uzzi Tuzii, it is eternally suspended between "the necessity to interject glosses on multiple meanings in the text and the awareness that all interpretation is a use of violence and caprice against" it. In his new novel, Calvino nevertheless breaks through this paralysis of bad faith in ways that have not yet been mentioned. If he exposes in his obsession with print his conflicting desire to reach whatever is beyond it, he also departs from the narrative point of view of author-centered metafiction, appealing directly to a community of individual readers—readers who are evidently for Calvino the resistance movement of our time, in the post-structuralist sense that they *are* the world.

While writer's block threatens to choke the book off at its source, *If on a Winter's Night* is really about the act of reading. Although shadowed by Roland Barthes, it is indebted most to the later Barthes of *S/Z* (1970) and, especially, *The Pleasure of the Text* (1973), his lyrical meditation on the erotics of reading the decentered or reader-written text of "bliss." In the frame story, and from the first word, an undisguised, historically existing "Calvino" courts the reader by telling it from "your" point of view: "You are about to begin reading Italo Calvino's new novel, *If on a Winter's Night a Traveler.* Relax. Concentrate." He extends the tradition of the directly addressed "Dear Reader" into a present-tense, second-person discourse. From the first word, "you" are referred to as the hero of this novel, by right of your having chosen it, opened it, and thus resisted alternatives, especially the attractions of the mass media: "Best to close the door; the TV is always on in the next room." As deconstructing reader, you are on the one hand distinguishable from the text and, on the other, personified into "your story." Thus literalized, "you" are singled out—as Calvino stresses the "heterogeneity of readers and works" according to post-structuralist theory. Calvino in turn is what "you" make him. In a gesture of resignation of authorial presence—a hard one to pull off—"Calvino" allows "you" to note the absence of his "unmistakeable" tone: "No. You Don't recognize it at all. But now that you think about it, who ever said that this author had an unmistakeable tone?"

This romance-with-the reader gimmick may seem rather too cutely extracted from Barthes, as it is at least partly intended to. But in erasing the characterized narrator, Calvino theoretically "decenters" the text; he overleaps the barrier of the authoritarian "I" which is the limit of the "frigid," orally fixated, "prattling" text, as Barthes calls it, and to whom the reader is "nothing except [an] address." What to think of this "Mobius strip of a new twist on literary self-consciousness," as John Updike puts the issue, is left up to the omnipotent reader.

Another twist is on the postmodern convention of foregrounding. Instead of reducing the story to text and commentary, Calvino brings the text to life, for instance, dramatizing the deconstruction process as a confusion of the reading experience with the imagined world it projects. The first pseudonovel "begins in a railway station, a locomotive huffs, steam from a piston covers the opening of the chapter, a cloud of smoke hides part of the first paragraph." The page is "clouded like the windows of an old train, the cloud of smoke rests on the sentences." And yet, as often as the image moves toward the sentence or page, the reverse occurs; the text naturalizes itself. In the second "novel," "An odor of frying wafts at the opening of the page, of onion in fact, onion being fried." Soon pages, margins, and nuances all are "enveloped in the smell of simmering oil."

Much as the smell of frying onions erases the print, the "I" of the last "novel" erases the oppressive urban skyline. And so, alluding to the characteristic texture and theme of his neo-realistic phase, Calvino passes his wand over the clutter of signs that we call the world and erases it, substituting images that palpably suspend between reality and the void:

I feel the need to reduce [an ornate ministry building] to a smooth vertical surface, a slab of opaque glass, a partition that defines space without imposing itself on one's sight. . . . I decide to do away with it completely; . . . a milky sky rises over the bare ground. The world is so complicated, tangled, and overloaded that to see into it with any clarity you must prune and prune.

Mary McCarthy notes a similar erasure in the pseudo-novels; they are not parodies; they hint at "faint resemblances . . . so evanescent that they cannot be pinned down." Calvino plays on our conflicting desires to read obliviously and also to name the type, allowing neither, tantalizing us along. Thus led, we discover the book's principle in the diary of Silas Flannery: "I would like . . . to write a book that is only an *incipit*, that maintains for its whole duration the potentiality of the beginning, the expectation still not focused on an object." Through his unfolding series of *incipits*, Calvino draws the reader into the text only to erase it, making it in effect "yours," and so propelling "you" beyond it, into a world "somewhere beyond the book, beyond the author, beyond the conventions of writing" toward a voice "from the unsaid, from what the world has not yet said of itself and does not yet have the words to say." Each of the ten beginnings leads "you," in pursuit of the text, to the spaces that the text exists to open up—to Switzerland and Flannery, to Professor Uzzi Tuzii or back to the bookseller—and ultimately to Ludmilla, the Other Reader.

"In a world where our lives are circumscribed by governments, unions, armies, and politicians that paralyze us more than help us, Calvino relies finally on the individual voice," asserts Frank MacShane. Perhaps "voice" should be altered slightly to "reader" and singular to plural. For "Calvino's" courting of the reader is complemented, and finally overshadowed, by the Reader's courting of the Other Reader, Ludmilla, who is of course the mysterious reading woman. Sister of the computer-obsessed Lotaria, prototype of readers "who use books to produce other books," Ludmilla is the naive reader, for whom reading is "the current that brings the sentences to graze the filter of her attention, to stop for a moment before being absorbed by the circuits of her mind and disappearing, transformed into her interior ghosts, into what in her is most personal and incommunicable."

Ludmilla's "common" reading is meant to be the least simple, most vital, and most inter-communicative of activities. In *The Pleasure of the Text*, Barthes evokes in similar terms the "best pleasure," which is also the process through which his "best ideas" are generated. The text "makes itself heard indirectly; I am led to look up often, to listen to something else" in an "act that is slight, complex, tenuous, almost scatterbrained: a sudden movement of the head like a bird who understands nothing of what we hear, who hears what we do not understand."

Such a Barthesian reading of Barthes is behind Calvino's seventh chapter, in which "your" romance with Ludmilla develops into yet another kind of naive reading—complicated by the real reader's awareness of its taking place. Calvino literalizes Barthes' "kitchen of meaning" as "you" decipher Ludmilla's apartment, finding "bare walls here, crammed ones there," suggesting a "need to concentrate signs into a kind of dense script, surrounded by the void in which to find repose and refreshment again." A "certain aesthetic tendency" is noticeable in "a panoply of half-moon choppers, in decreasing sizes," and its opposite, "ropes of garlic hung within reach," telling of a relationship with food "not careless or generic." And suddenly, just as the real reader begins to forget the textual nature of these pleasures, a rivalry emerges between "you" and "Calvino," who for the first time, becomes "I," making Ludmilla the intimately addressed "tu," and you-the-Reader a third person—until "Calvino" relents and . . . "you" may read Ludmilla's body as she in turn skims your "index," but the real reader is now forever conscious of an invisible voyeur.

In this momentary demonstration of Authorial presence, the source of Flannery's and Marana's rivalry for the Other Reader, Calvino alerts "you" to the hard fact that this consummation is a transaction initiated by the writer. Even so, the intrusion reminds the real reader of the Author's previous absence, of his yielding of beginnings over to the active reader for completion. Reading is thus made comparable to existential becoming.

As John Gardner has said, for Calvino existence is "an act of will confirmed by love." His existentialism in Camusian terms is that of *The Plague* rather than *The Stranger*, its emphasis on contingency as opposed to solipsism. The primary analogy throughout *If on a Winter's Night* is therefore, as in Barthes' *Pleasure of the Text*, between reading and lovemaking, if with a significantly different emphasis. Barthes' analogy is suggested throughout, especially in the attentive, seductive rhythm of Calvino's prose as it moves between text and context. The point on which Calvino differs is dramatized in the Reader's romance with the Other Reader. Without that romance, this mere "second-person discourse" (and, by implication, Barthes's lyrical meditation) is suspect, as "Calvino" admits, even asserts: "you" may well be "brother and double of a hypocrite I," an imaginary friend. For a novel, "at least two yous are required, distinct and concomitant," and between whom something can "take form, develop, or deteriorate according to the phases of human events."

The *menage à trois* is therefore necessary to open a space for the Other Reader, so that the novel can properly begin. According to the narrator, "What makes lovemaking and reading resemble each other most is that within both of them times and spaces open, different from measureable time and space." It is in these passages, Calvino hopes, that solitary readers give and take, that "the voice of that silent nobody made of ink and typographical spacing can become yours and hers, a language, a code between the two of you, a means to exchange signals and recognize each other." To reflect the way real novels work, Calvino says in effect, the phenomenology of reading must be extended to include the sharing of reader responses, or the context that interacting readers create. For this reason, as early as the thirty-second page, reading has become a dialogue between readers, "an instrument, a channel of communication, a rendezvous." "Calvino" asks rhetorically, "What is more natural than a solidarity, a complicity, a bond should be established between Reader and Reader, thanks to the book?" The book ends in "your" (plural) marriage, a commitment to the common activity and (yes) cause of reading. In the final chapter a "great double bed" receives your "parallel readings." Therefore, if for Calvino civilization rests on the individual act of reading, that is because reading, however solitary when taking place, is finally realized as a transaction, a social act.

Barthes' *The Pleasure of the Text* is Calvino's main gimmick in *If on a Winter's Night a Traveler*, but this is more than a parody or tour de force. It stretches Barthes' lyrical (and thus intransitive) meditations toward their conclusions to show how reading's erotic dimensions extend to social and political realms. In doing so, Calvino corrects Barthes, whose own text of bliss is circularly and hedonistically auto-erotic—addressed really (in the modernist author-centered mode that goes back at least as far as Baudelaire) to himself as ideal reader. Calvino does agree with Barthes that reading, like erotic pleasure, "cannot be taken over by any collectivity, mentality, or ideolect," depending as it does on a logic of sensation and being a "drift, something both revolutionary and asocial." But Calvino goes on to pose a post-structuralist resolution to the quarrel between formalism and Marxism, a resolution that Barthes attempts but never convincingly reaches. Calvino dramatizes the dialectic through which *poiesis* is realized in *praxis*, or the process through which a text becomes a medium of engagement. The novel as exemplified in *If on a Winter's Night* is to be considered a site for the transformation of ideologies, the "social process of culture" which takes place, as Tony Bennett says, "not within texts but between texts, and between texts and readers; not some ideal, disembodied reader; but historically concrete readers."

Calvino's romance with the reader begins as he dramatizes, through postmodernist conventions, a deconstructionist theory which can tend toward voyeurism or even solipsism. However, through the mediation or medium of "you," a historical reader, the book generates a love affair, a transaction with the world outside itself. The romance ends as the text becomes a context for a heterogeneous, if also collective activity—thus the titles of the pseudonovels *In a network of lines that enlace* and *In a network of lines that intersect*. The penultimate chapter eleven surveys the dismaying diversity of readers' responses, to resolve in the seventh reader's allusion to the fact behind their solidarity: "The ultimate meaning to which all stories refer has two faces: the continuity of life, the inevitability of death." It is then, in "a flash," after reflecting on these words, that "you decide you want to marry Ludmilla." The marriage thus refers the individual reader to the community that partly determines it. It is this community of individual, parallel readers "out there" or underground, that resists, however passively and privately, formulation and system—the tyranny of plots, propaganda, the codes built into the text itself, Marana's literature of bad faith. The reading resistance takes shape out of the play of dialogue among readers, out of their incessant transformation of signs into new signifiers, an exchange which in its infinite variety defeats what Barthes calls "*the* exchange," the collective economy which "our modernity makes a constant effort to defeat." When people are reading, as even Marana has to admit, "something happens over which I have no power." This happening, as the government censor (a closet reader) goes on to explain, "is the limit that even the most omnipotent police force cannot broach. We can prevent reading: but in the decree that forbids reading there will be still read something of the truth that we would wish never to be read."

The Sensual Philosopher: Mr. Palomar

Symmetries and arithmetics have always tempted Italo Calvino's imagination to grow flirtatious and to begin its fantastic displays. Early on, he gave us some marvelous binary blarney in his tale *The Cloven Viscount*, a dual patterning of good and evil, a two-storied story that opened as fluently and knowingly as a zipper in a penthouse. That same allegorical impulse operated with equal freedom but with even more archness and architectural invention in *Invisible Cities*. Then came the cat's cradle narrations of *The Castle of Crossed Destinies*, regulated but not determined by the inner relations of the cards in the tarot deck. Now we ask ourselves, can he possibly get away with it again?

Mr. Calvino's new book has three main sections entitled "Mr. Palomar's Vacation," "Mr. Palomar in the City" and "The Silences of Mr. Palomar." Each main section has three subsections and each subsection three parts and Mr. Calvino has created a numbering system for them. "The numbers 1, 2, 3 that mark the titles of the index," he writes,

> whether they are in the first, second, or third position, besides having a purely ordinal value, correspond also to three thematic areas, three kinds of experience and inquiry that, in varying proportions are present in every part of the book.

From *The New York Times* (29 September 1985). © 1985 New York Times Company.

Those marked "1" generally correspond to a visual experience. . . .

Those marked "2" contain elements that are anthropological, or cultural in the broad sense. . . .

Those marked "3" involve more speculative experience, concerning the cosmos, time, infinity, the relationship between the self and the world. ⟨Translation by William Weaver⟩

But can this tongue that stays so neutrally in its cheek as it explains the book's structural principles woo us into pleasure and assent all over again in the actual text?

Happily, the schema turns out to be not just a prescription; what might have been for a lesser imagination a grid acts in this case like a springboard, and indeed one suspects anyhow that the numerological stuff evolved from the accidents of composition and not vice versa. Each of these pieces has the feel of a single inspiration being caught as it rises and then being played for all its life is worth—though not for an instant longer than it takes to exhaust its first energy.

Mr. Palomar is a lens employed by his author in order to inspect the phenomena of the world, but the lens is apt to turn into a mirror which reflects the hesitations and self-corrections of Mr. Palomar's own reflecting mind. The book consists of a graduated sequence of descriptions and speculations in which the protagonist confronts the problem of discovering his place in the world and of watching those discoveries dissolve under his habitual intellectual scrutiny.

So the very first movement is entitled "Reading a Wave" and here Mr. Palomar attempts to see and describe and kidnap into language the exact nature of a single wave. His precisions, which he must keep revising, are constantly accurate and constantly inadequate; yet it is these very frustrations which constitute the reader's pleasure. By the last movement, however, Mr. Palomar has turned his gaze inward and is now, as the title of the piece puts it, "Learning to Be Dead." But his appetite for certain knowledge remains equally tantalized and unsatisfied: "You must not confuse being dead with not being." In between there are other 25 texts which one hesitates to call prose poems since it makes them sound much too affected and humorless, or meditations, since that undersells their lovely metaphorical ease and rapture.

Mr. Calvino's line whispers and lazes and tautens and sports itself very cajolingly. His gaze, like Mr. Palomar's as he contemplates the stars, "remains alert, available, released from all certitude." "In August," he tells us, "the Milky Way assumes a dense consistency, and you might say it is overflowing its bed." The lavish simplicity of that, its double gratitude for the world and for words adequate to the world, its mingled sense of something sweetly and personally discovered yet also something of almost racial memory, this atmosphere of spacious and buoyant reverie is typical of the whole work.

Here is a large unhampered talent sailing a middle course between the sophistication of the avant-garde and the innocence of the primitive poetic imagination, between the kind of intelligence that constructed the medieval bestiaries and the preliterate intuitiveness that once chanted hunters' prayers. If the persona of Mr. Palomar is haunted at times by the petulant shade of Molloy in Samuel Beckett's play, trying to devise an infallible method by which to rotate his sucking stones from pocket to mouth to pocket, and at other times by the urbane Jorge Luis Borges, softly expatiating upon the question of whether writing gets done by "Borges" or "I," the reader is not worried. Nor is Mr. Calvino. He knows that everybody ends up worrying about the same things anyhow.

Mr. Palomar worries and watches incessantly and in Italian; but William Weaver has me persuaded that I now know his fastidious, easily beguiled and graciously implacable mind in English. The rhythms and savors of Mr. Weaver's language can render equally well the punctilio of Mr. Palomar's intellectual searches and the civility and eroticism of his daydreams. It is a language that brings us nearer that destination which Mr. Palomar constantly aspires to—"a step closer to true knowledge, which lies in the experience of the flavors, composed of memory and imagination at once."

> Behind every cheese, [he muses] there is a pasture of a different green under a different sky: meadows caked with salt that the tides of Normandy deposit every evening; meadows scented with aromas in the windy sunlight of Provence; there are different flocks, with their stablings and their transhumances; there are secret processes handed down over the centuries. This shop is a museum: Mr. Palomar, visiting it, feels as he does in the Louvre, behind every displayed object the presence of the civilization that has given it form and takes form from it.

Nevertheless, for all its sensual felicity, the writing is philosophically impelled. Mr. Palomar, who takes his name from the famous telescope and observatory, is both an "I" and an "eye," "A world looking at the world," as the title of one of Mr. Palomar's meditations suggests, a question mark retroactively affecting his own credibility: "Is he not a piece of the world that is looking at another piece of the world? Or else, given that there is world that side of the window and world this side, perhaps the 'I,' the ego, is simply the window through which the world looks at the world. To look at itself, the world needs the eyes (and the eyeglasses) of Mr. Palomar."

Which mercifully takes us, Mr. Palomar and Italo Calvino beyond the impasse of solipsism, the distrust of language and the frigid fires of "experiment." There may be a problem of knowledge, but the consciousness only comes alive to this problem by suffering those constant irrepressible appetites for experience which want to rampage beyond the prison of the self. Mr. Calvino may divide and categorize in triplicate the visual, the cultural and the speculative aspects of Mr. Palomar's world, he may prompt and tag and analyze and juxtapose to his (and our) heart's content, but Mr. Palomar himself remains wonderfully spontaneous and receptive to the pell-mell of the senses. Lawns, breasts, starlings, planets, lizards, the moon in the afternoon, the blackbird's whistle, the clack of mating tortoises, the fog of memories in "Two Pounds of Goose Fat" where "in the thick, soft whiteness that fills the jars, the clangor of the world is muffled"—all these things and a thousand others keep the mind from its ultimate shadow feast. Mr. Palomar may collapse at the end, like the book named for him, in a syllogism, but not before he has outstripped his conclusion in one incandescent apotheosis after another.

If it often seems in the course of this book that Mr. Calvino cannot put a foot wrong, this is because he is not a pedestrian writer. Like Robert Frost, his whole concern is for himself as a performer, but whereas Frost performed at eye-level, as it were, on vocal cords and heartstrings, Mr. Calvino is on the high wires, on lines of thought strung out above the big international circus. Yet such high-wire displays engage us only if the performer is in fact subject to gravity and genuinely at risk. A lightweight can throw the same shapes but cannot evince that old, single, open-mouthed stare of hope and wonder which we all still want to be a part of. What is most impressive about *Mr. Palomar* is a sense of the safety net being withdrawn at the end, of beautiful, nimble, solitary feats of imagination being carried off not so much to dazzle an audience as to outface what the poet Philip Larkin calls "the solving emptiness / That lies just under all we do."

JOHN DOLIS

Calvino's Cosmicomics: *Original Si(g)n*

Modern science generally thinks it has the upper hand. George Sarton professes the common belief: "The history of science might be defined as the history of the discovery of objective truth, of the gradual conquest of matter by the human mind." In this holy war, science pretends that it enlists the aid of technology, which, since the Renaissance, has come to be conceived as science's handmaid(en)—one, indeed, who, like the submissive subordinate, dutifully performs the dirty work of the maid(en). Let's dismiss this myth at the outset. In "reality," its "truth" (the master-slave relationship) is reversed. Science is nothing if not—has never been anything but—the servant of technology. Its will to power emerges in the very space of this repression, the space where science draws the line between "fiction" ("making," "construction," "invention"—i.e., techne) and "fact" (the product of disinterest, "divorce"—i.e., observation). At the heart of this (mis)construction of "reality" resides the subject-object dichotomy whose maidenly handiwork now sanitizes the object, anaesthetizes it, sterilizes it, redeems it from the subject's dirty hands.

Particle physics, however, has undermined the strength of science's manipulation of, its strangle-hold on, "reality." Quantum reality, as a whole, exceeds the possibility of representation: its "truth" inhabits the boundaries of subjectivity itSelf. As Allen C. Dotson observes, "we can no longer

From *Extrapolation* 39, no. 1 (Spring 1998). © 1998 by the Kent State University Press.

assume, when we ascribe properties to, say, a proton, that in any meaningful sense we are discussing attributes that it possesses independent of any measurement process that may or may not be underway"; in other words, "there is no objectively real linkage proposed between a proton and a measurement apparatus." According to the principle of complementarity, "there is no reality until that reality is perceived." This (im)position relocates "truth": it signals the marriage of subject and object, appearance and reality. In "reality," they've never been divorced.

The discourse of quantum physics thus begins the story of the end of truth, its fiction, the fiction of truth. Truth isn't stranger than fiction; it is (a) fiction: it bears the mark of discourse, of signification, in light of (the "fact" of) its meaning. As with any "story," there must be a narrator. Quantum theory recites the subject (the observer) at the site of truth: it signals the truth of fiction. Here discourse locates the story of (the "truth" of) reality in a dimension other than the object alone, a reality whose "matter" returns every-"thing" to fabrication, technique, technology (techne)—the subject (matter) itSelf. As quantum discourse puts it, the observer is part of the event. Reality arises in this margin of manipulation: it signifies the space in which Calvino hands us over to the co(s)mic, the inverse of the universe—the way in which his fiction stands the universal (objectivity) on its head (subjectivity), manhandles things, reverses things, turns things upside-down. The "thing" (res), as Heidegger suggests, is nothing but a "matter" of discourse.

Cosmicomics articulates this state of affairs and its ironic inversion: now matter itself "speaks," speaks of "itself." Narration will remark the space of its appearance: narration matters; it makes the universe appear, its disparate episodes linked by a single narrative consciousness, Qfvfq, that "recalls," "remembers" each of the book's thirteen separate stories. Observation is therefore set on its head—subject and object, observer and observed, upended. Calvino reverses the quantum wholeness of "the world" according to particle physics: the observed becomes the observer. Given to discourse, the universe hence opens onto time, emerges to consciousness, to history, a story of its own, a story that recounts how every "thing" (res) is part of the whole yet subject to observation, including the observation of itself. Thus Qfvfq recounts things from the beginning, "the moment when all the universe's matter was concentrated in a single point, before it began to expand in space." Narration, here, is universal, always already "there," self-constitutive—like Tristram Shandy, in on its own "conception." *Cosmicomics* makes timely this event, remembers the universe, reflects the universal. Matter consequently comes to life, acquires a life of its own, its life a book, a story whose various characters range from atoms and cellular structures to mollusks and dinosaurs, each, in its way, "a particle of truth," each recounting its universal significance, the way in which it matters to the universe—bequeaths to it the very time of its life.

So too, the narrative consciousness of *Cosmicomics* belongs to the universal. This consciousness, whose identity falls under the sign that names it, whose name goes under the sign Qfvfq, is subject to signification in ways identical to those that govern the behavior of the particle. Here nothing operates in a vacuum: where something is, there's always something else, something other. From its inception, moreover, its point of origin, both particle and consciousness remove themselves from the whole of (their) being—that is, Being as a whole. The whole now lies beyond, outside, space (and time)—the event of Being prior to its own advent—and functions as the origin of myth: the myth of origins. Regarding matter as a whole, the Big Bang articulates this logic, as Qfvfq observes, "Naturally, we were all there, . . . where else could we have been? Nobody knew then that there could be space. Or time either: what use did we have for time, packed in there like sardines? I say 'packed like sardines,' using a literary image: in reality there wasn't even space to pack us into. Every point of each of us coincided with every point of each of the others in a single point, which was where we all were."

Consciousness understands its origins under the rubrics of a similar logic. Here too, something—the subject as a (w)hole—emerges from nothing, a nothing that somehow always already contains everything ahead of itself. This "spaceless," "massless" nothing that precedes the subject, and by means of which the subject is given over to itSelf, goes under the sign of "language"—whose signified itself remarks an arbitrary system of signs. The chronology of this event demands a cause/effect relation: either humans invented language or it preceded subjectivity. Qfvfq sets out the depth of this abyss: "once . . . I drew a sign at a point in space, just so I could find it again two hundred million years later [the time it takes the sun to make a complete revolution of the galaxy], when we went by the next time around. What sort of a sign? It's hard to explain because . . . in that period I didn't have any examples to follow, . . . there were no things to copy. . . . In other words, considering it was the first sign ever made in the universe, or at least in the circuit of the Milky Way, I must admit it came out very well." While all other points in space were indistinguishable, this one now "had the sign on it." The problem of inside/outside already appears, and Qfvfq concedes that the sign stays still, remains, because he "leaned over the border of the Galaxy a little." Indeed, its initial significance as referent depends upon the "outside" of this "remainder." The object as such—that is, the object (mis)taken as "the Real"—is an outsider: always already beyond the subject itSelf.

With this event, being opens onto reflection, (re)turns to its self: "I couldn't think about anything else; . . . to think something had never been possible, first because there were no things to think about, and second because signs to think of them by were lacking, but . . . [now] it was possible for someone thinking to think of a sign, and therefore that one, in the sense that the sign was the thing you could think about and also the sign of the thing thought, namely, itself." This paradox recuperates duplicity, the double edge of its incision in logic: the chicken/egg dilemma is chronologically beyond the aegis of "truth." If subjectivity requires the sign to think, then how can it "invent" the sign in "the first place"? In order to do so would require, in turn, that the subject already thinks, already possesses the very sign it would create. Simultaneity accommodates, at best, an onto-logical priority. The question of (self) identity emerges in this margin as well: "at the same time that sign was mine, the sign of me. . . . It was like a name, the name of that point, and also my name that I had signed on the spot. . . . I carried it with me, it inhabited me, possessed me entirely."

Waiting for its return, however, solicits its very disappearance, fading from consciousness: "though I recalled its general outline, . . . still something about it eluded me." Unable to derive any further signs and their combinations "because that first sign was missing as a term of comparison," Qfvfq abides the galactic circuit, anticipating the return of the origin(al). In its place, however, there appears only "a shapeless scratch, a bruised, chipped abrasion of space. . . . Space, without a sign, was once again a chasm, the void." The origin can only return as a ghost—other than itself. Light years pass, and Qfvfq sees once again a sign, "a sign unquestionably copied from mine, . . . a wretched counterfeit of . . . that sign whose ineffable purity I could only now—through contrast—recapture." A "plurimillennial chain of deductions" produces the following scenario: "on another planetary system which performed its galactic revolution before us, there was a certain Kgwgk . . . consumed with envy, who had erased my sign in a vandalistic impulse and then, with vulgar artifice, had attempted to make another." The sign (re)turns the subject to being other than itSelf.

The Other now marks the propagation of the sign, that duplicitous space that makes a difference. The advent of signification (to) itSelf. The birth of universal significance: "the world . . . was beginning to produce an image of itself." A universe of signs remarks the signs of a universe. Now too, the sign of the Other enables Qfvfq to (re)sign himSelf: "in this new sign of mine you could perceive the influence of our new way of looking at things, call it style if you like." Hence, subjectivity is given to its own design. In the space of this transformation, moreover, time emerges to being—the mark by means of which the subject differs from itSelf, is always already belated, untimely, passé: "I had left that sign in space . . . which now, in my memory, seemed inappropriate, in all its pretension, a sign chiefly of an antiquated way of conceiving signs . . . . In other words, I was ashamed of that sign which went on through the centuries, being passed by worlds in flight, making a ridiculous spectacle of itself and of me." Similarly, any sign is subject to this risk, resigning the subject to (an) unfashionable design: "a sign that now might seem perfect to me, in two hundred or six hundred million years would make me look absurd. Instead, in my nostalgia, the first sign, brutally rubbed out by Kgwgk, remained beyond the attacks of time . . . Making signs that weren't that sign no longer held any interest for me."

In this event, foreclosed from the truth of his original si(g)n, Qfwfq goes in for making "false" signs—"notches in space, holes, stains"—that Kgwgk nevertheless continues to erase. After the passage of innumerable galactic years, it little pleases Qfwfq that these erasures begin to fade. Returning his original sign to "pristine visibility" becomes its own impossibility: "space was no longer that uniformly barren and colorless expanse. The idea of fixing with signs the points where we passed . . . had occurred to many. . . . So it happened that I reached the point of my sign, and I found five, all there. And I wasn't able to recognize my own." With this proliferation, the world and space become "the mirror of each other." Signs establish a continuity with no precise boundaries: "now there was no longer a container and a thing contained, but only a general thickness of signs superimposed and coagulated, occupying the whole volume of space . . . . There was no longer any way to establish a point of reference"; now "any point could be the point of departure." That is to say, space is nothing but this configuration of signs; the very space of the sign is but the sign of space. As Qfwfq remarks, "it was clear that, independent of signs, space didn't exist and perhaps had never existed." At the level of matter, the particle itself procures this space. As Heisenberg expressed it, atoms are not things. The particle is not a thing, but an event: it signals where being "takes place." The real is not found on the hither side of its appearance. It belongs to the appearance as such. If, in its infancy, modern (Newtonian) physics imagined reality as a plenum or phallus, filling (the [w]hole of) "Mother" Nature through and through, quantum physics repeats the (dis)content of this empty (primal) scene, this interpretive infelicity: what never "took place"—took up space—as such. Quantum reality is not objective in the sense of being "out there" (in-itself); rather, it is a ghostly reality able to "inhabit" an infinite number of places at the same time: a quantum wave function. Just as Schroedinger's equation spelled the end of representation, Heisenberg's Uncertainty Principle marked the demise of "reality" understood as wholly present to itself. Regarding its observation—that is, measuring position and momentum—the path of the particle "comes into existence only when we observe it." Here being and meaning are one and the same—emerge within the space of signification. Thus, Fred Alan Wolf suggests, "no clear dividing line exists between ourselves and the reality we observe to exist outside ourselves. Instead, reality depends upon our choices of what and how we choose to observe." The particle not only cites the place where subject and object intersect; it signals their complicity. Reality takes place at the site of observation. Both subject and object become each other's citation. Similarly, the particle—a photon, for example—recites reality in (the) place of its (dis)appearance—the point at which the quantum wave function collapses. Reality is neither "in" the subject nor "in" the object, but in their relation: "the universe is not just a collection of separate points. It is what it is according to the observer. . . . By identifying with the 'quantum wholeness' of the world, the observer 'becomes' the observed. He is what he sees." Appearance and disappearance are part of one and the same event.

So too, Qfvfq "appears" only in light of Kgwgk's erasures. This correspondence between being and meaning suggests the way in which the signifier transforms subjectivity to discourse. In the language of Lacan, a signifier represents a subject for another signifier. It's not by chance such correspondence recuperates a primal scene, repeats or, to use Kierkegaard's terminology, "recollects forward" the Freudian fort-da. The "space" of Qfvfq's "original" sign now re(a)sembles the space of repression. Meaning arises from this violent gap—the gap in signification by means of which the (self)reflexive subject reveals its origin in the Other, that boundary or limit of the subject as signifier (of desire), the very structure of its lack. Here Qfvfq's absent sign makes present the (w)hole it would fill, the void of (its own) space: meaning "takes place" prior to being, displaces being with its ghost. Qfvfq's circuit and return enact the way in which this missing (primal) scene—"another locality, another space," the encounter (tuche) in as much as it is missed, "in so far as it is essentially the missed encounter" inhabits the very place we would expect to see appear that locus of the "real."

Cosmicomics recites this "form of space," the (dis)content of this empty scene, this interpretive infelicity (what never "took place" as such), when, falling through "the void" with Ursula H'x and Lieutenant Fenimore, Qfvfq discovers its "out"-line, the way its internal figures configure its external shape, the immanent relation between within and without: "so the pimple growing on a caliph's nose or the soap bubble resting on a laundress's bosom changes the general form of space in all its dimensions." While the grain of space is "porous and broken with crevasses and dunes," its general properties are such that "one parallel went one way, and another in another way." Thus, "What you might consider straight, one-dimensional lines were similar, in effect, to lines of handwriting made on a white page by a pen that shifts words and fragments of sentences from one line to another, with insertions and cross-references, in the haste to finish an exposition which has gone through successive, approximate drafts, always unsatisfactory."

In the same way, falling through space, Qfwfq observes that Lieutenant Fenimore and he pursued each other, "hiding behind the loops of the I's, especially the l's of the word 'parallel,' in order to shoot and take cover from the bullets"—or that he might seize Ursula H'x by the hair, "and bend her against a *d* or a *t* just as I write them now, in haste, bent, so you can recline against them." These same lines, however, might be reconfigured just as easily: "rather than remain series of letters and words, can easily be drawn out in their black thread and unwound in continuous, parallel, straight lines which mean nothing beyond themselves in their constant flow, never meeting, just as we never meet in our constant fall: I, Ursula H'x, and Lieutenant Fenimore, and all the others." Here, under the figure of "falling" (Heidegger's not far away), writing inscribes the void of subjectivity, that missed encounter ("never meeting") being beside itSelf. This structure mirrors the space of both particle and consciousness alike.

Just as there is no reality "outside" the world of signs, so too there's nothing noumenal beyond the phenomenon. The purity, the transparency, of an original sign is irrecoverable simply because it never existed in "the first place." Meaning arises in (the) place of contamination, the desire of the other. Similarly, there is no "other" side to reality beyond the appearance, no hidden meaning, no secret message revealing a transparent picture of the whole. As Bell's theorem suggests, if hidden parameters exist, they must show themselves: there are no hidden variables. Consciousness merely creates them whenever it seeks a reality not there: "Since there is nothing out there until we find it, we are discovering nothing more than ourselves. No wonder we find paradox wherever we look." Subjectivity is that very nothing it seeks: consciousness—itSelf—this hidden parameter. The sign always already harbors this event.

Qfwfq sets out its structure in light of the structure of light. One night, observing the sky with his telescope, he notices a sign, "hanging from a galaxy a hundred million light years away. On it was written: I SAW YOU." This dates the observation itself to two hundred million (light) years ago. Even before he checks his diary, he's seized by the presentiment that at that very moment "something had happened to me that I had always tried to hide." At first, he would reply with a sign like "LET ME EXPLAIN," but then thinks it best to put up something to the effect, "LET'S SEE IF YOU'RE TELLING THE TRUTH: WHAT WAS I DOING?" He finally opts for the simple, "WHAT OF IT?"

He further reasons that, if they had seen him that day, they likewise saw him on all the following ones, and would therefore modify their initial negative opinion. In the nights to follow, however, he observes similar signs from other distant galaxies, "as if in the space containing all the galaxies the image of what I had done that day were being projected in the interior of a sphere that swelled constantly, at the speed of light." With this, another realization comes to haunt him: "At a certain point the farthest galaxies that had seen me (or had seen the I SAW YOU sign from a galaxy closer to us, or the I SAW THE I SAW YOU from a bit further on) would reach the ten-billion-light-year threshold, beyond which they would move off at three hundred thousand kilometers per second, the speed of light, and no image would be able to overtake them after that. So there was the risk that . . . their temporary mistaken opinion . . . would become definitive . . . beyond all appeal and therefore, in a sense, correct, corresponding to truth." A further intuition appeases Qfvfq for the moment. The later, positive images of his behavior will overtake the most distant, fastest galaxies so that they take this definitive image with them beyond time and space, "where it would become the truth containing in its sphere with unlimited radius all the other spheres with their partial and contradictory truths."

At last the moment arrives, the night upon which might come back to him from that initial galaxy a recognition of his later, positive behavior. A sign appears: "TRA-LA-LA-LA." Proof of himSelf goes by unobserved, as Qfvfq concludes, because someone "allowed himself five minutes of idleness, of relaxation, we might as well say of irresponsibility." It's not for nothing that Qfvfq conceives of his own identity in terms of its dependence upon another—the other's ability to respond, to signal back. In this regard, he harbors a final hope that other galaxies will testify, bear witness, to his imaginary ideal, the ideal image of himSelf. On successive nights, other signs appear: "YOU HAVE A FLANNEL UNDERSHIRT," for example, and "THAT CHARACTER'S REALLY ON THE BALL WHO THE HELL CAN HE BE?" That is, others either fail to observe him, miss him entirely, or—what amounts to the same thing—fail to recognize him when he appears. With this, Qfvfq loses heart: "Those who had seen me had seen me in a partial, fragmentary, careless way . . . missing the essential quality." Consciousness thus resembles a particle, behaves similarly. On the hither side of its behavior, there is no "essential quality." In any case, that essential quality missing is (nothing but) significance itself, meaning missing (from) itSelf. Space constitutes the place where subject and object coalesce, that vicinity in which "objectivity" (the particle as "referent," as [the] Real) (dis)appears, that locality where consciousness comes upon the scene (primal, if you will) in "the first place." Qfvfq cannot return to this (non)event because it never happened. Consciousness cannot recover itSelf, cannot recuperate its loss(es), just as the particle forcloses its past. The wave collapses with observation, vanishes for every particular consciousness—indeed, has always already deserted the very scene of its own scenario. ⟨As Fred A. Wolf writes in *Taking the Quantum Leap,*⟩ "The wave is not the ultimate reality. The particle is not the ultimate reality. Reality is not the ultimate reality. There is, instead, one unbroken wholeness that appears paradoxical as soon as we observers attempt to analyze it. . . . To Bohr, there was no wave to collapse unless the wave was observed, and then no collapse would be seen. He viewed analysis as observation, and observation was fundamentally a discontinuous event. It could not be connected to any past occurrence. The connection with the past was not a reality."

In the same way, Qfvfq's efforts to retrieve the past are ultimately futile: by definition, it "lies" in ruins, the shadow of itSelf: "no action of mine, good or bad, was completely lost. At least an echo of it was always saved; or rather several echoes . . .; but the echoes were discontinous, conflicting pieces of information, inessential." Thus he directs himSelf toward the future, a gesture equally futile: "I procured an enormous directional sign, one of those huge hands with the pointing index finger. When I performed an action to which I wanted to call attention, I had only to raise that sign, trying to make the finger point at the most important detail of the scene. For the moments when . . . I preferred not to be observed, I made another sign, a hand with the thumb pointing in the direction opposite the one I was turning, to distract attention." It comes as no surprise that he discovers, too late, "I should have pointed out what I hadn't wanted seen and should have hidden what I had instead pointed out."

Meanwhile, the galaxies approach their threshold: "one by one, they would disappear from the last ten-billion-light-year horizon beyond which no visible object can be seen, and they would bear with them a judgment by then irrevocable." Thinking of this final judgment, Qfvfq experiences a certain relief, "as if peace could come to me only after the moment when there would be nothing to add and nothing to remove . . . and the galaxies . . . , winding from the sphere of darkness, seemed to bring with them the only possible truth about myself, and I couldn't wait until all of them, one after the other, had followed this path." Thus, what Einstein called a "spooky action at a distance" describes not only the phantom reality of "nature" taken as an objective, independently existing whole, but the ghosts of subjectivity as well, the echo of that system of signs in which it is captured, in which it emerges to meaning and, therefore, being itSelf: "the labyrinth with the empty center, where the investigator meets only his own shadow . . . his own solutions to his own puzzles." If observation—or "measurement" to use the language of physics—exposes a reality foreclosed to representation (as a whole), it simultaneously exposes the immeasurable as such. Measurement must forfeit not only "what was" but "what will be" as well. "Nature" is not ek-static. Neither is the sign. In some incomprehensible, some strange, uncanny way, the sign is ontologically prior to subjectivity, is "in" at the origin, in "the first place" gives birth not only to space, but to (the) time (of the subject) itSelf. The nature of this "truth" which quantum physics provokes—and which the narrative consciousness of *Cosmicomics* recuperates—echoes the abyss of paradox. The nature of nature, its "essence," exceeds the laws of propositional logic. Reality is (this) fiction: the story of the advent of being in meaning. Collapsed upon itSelf, consciousness abides, endures (its) time, the space of (its own) reflexion. That system of signs called "language" reflects, takes to heart, the principle of complementarity, takes complementarity as its heart—its kern, invoking Freud's terminology, its heart of nonsense. This (dis)location (re)determines meaning. It marks the end of "truth" as a dimension of the metaphysical opposition between appearance and reality—and its implicit subject-object dichotomy. Truth here exceeds, transgresses, the logical space of the proposition confined between the margins of tautology and contradiction. The narrative world of *Cosmicomics* exposed its truth between two instances of discourse. The end of the "true" world beings with fable, with fabrication, with fiction. In Zarathustrian fashion, meaning is set adrift, whose drift reflects that very drift of "the world" in light of which things might thus appear in "the first place." Qfvfq's "fabulous" narrative universe locates a discourse wherein the drift of (the meaning of) the world exceeds all limits: the dissolution of subject and object "in reality." Indeed, this universe (fore) "tells" itSelf: "Yes, but at the beginning nobody knew it,"—Qfvfq explained,—"I mean, you could foretell it perhaps, but instinctively, by ear, guessing. I don't want to boast, but from the start I was willing to bet that there was going to be a universe." Truth but drifts along and within the chasm opened up by the sign, the possibilities of fabrication, the meandering ways that words might take in telling a story (of how the true world is always already a fable).

In the concluding "fable" of *Cosmicomics*, Qfvfq's final (trans)form(ation) recites him at the site of a mollusk, whose being might seem blindly confined, forever sequestered from the (outside) world, restricted to the space of a shell. Yet within and without do not conform to logic's "objective" demand: "Since the shell had a form, the form of the world was also changed, in the sense that now it included the form of the world as it had been without a shell plus the form of the shell." Reciprocally, from within, the mollusk—creating a shell of breathtaking beauty—opens up the possibility of vision itself. "Thanks to us . . . space became a visual field" by means of which others, intruders, "who had always turned a deaf ear to the vocation of form," now blindly become recipients of sight, "quietly taking on the easiest part: adapting their lazy, embryonic receptive organs to what there was to receive" so that "sight . . . was the sight that the others had of us." Perfecting that vision remains "another story." In this one, however, "all . . . around us, eyes were opening": eyes of "polyps and cuttlefish," of "bream and mullet," of "crayfish and lobsters," of "flies and ants," of seals, snails, gulls, "the frowning eyes of an underwater fisherman," and (through the lens of a spyglass) "a sea captain's eyes"—while "Framed by far-sighted lenses I feel on me the far-sighted eyes of a zoologist, trying to frame me in the eye of a Rolleiflex." In other words, Qfwfq tells us, "I had foreseen absolutely every-thing." Under the "telling" sign of Qfwfq's universe, every "thing" becomes a story; the thing matters: matter is (some thing) to be contested—the thing (res) a "matter of discourse." *Cosmicomics* reveals this truth (of [the] matter): it "knows its things." Here narration locates the truth of "the world" in a dimension other than logic's objective "fact," in a reality whose very form returns all fabrication (techne) to the fiction (poiesis) whence it originates— "our true element," Qfwfq concludes, in the final story of *Cosmicomics*, "which extends without shores, without boundaries." What Niels Bohr expressed, *Cosmicomics* "tells" best: "There are the trivial truths and the great truths. The opposite of a trivial truth is plainly false. The opposite of a great truth is also true."

MICHAEL WOOD

Hidden in the Distance: Reading Calvino Reading

Italo Calvino once wrote that he "spent more time with the books of others than with my own." He added, "I do not regret it." That must be an unusual remark for a writer to make, even (or especially) a writer who worked in a publishing house. We may think of Mr. Cavedagna in *If on a Winter's Night a Traveller,* who is described as "a little man, shrunken and bent," not because he is like that, or looks like that, or even because he seems to have emerged from a book where little men are always shrunken and bent. No: "He seems to have come from a world in which they still read books where you encounter 'little men, shrunken and bent.'"

It is Mr. Cavedagna who puts galley proofs on a table very gently, "as if the slightest jolt could upset the order of the printed letters." Much of Calvino's sense of literature lives in that small image, and not only of literature. "I still have the notion that to live in peace and freedom is a frail kind of good fortune that might be taken from me in an instant." An order may be a modest form of art, the model of the good society, or it may be thoroughly repressive. We don't always have the choice of orders, but we do have the choice of ways of thinking about them. "The ideal library," Calvino says, is one that gravitates towards the outside, toward the "apocryphal" books, in the etymological sense of the word: that is, "hidden" books. Literature is a search for the book hidden in the distance that alters the value and meaning

From *The Kenyon Review* 20, no. 2 (Spring 1998). © 1998 by Kenyon College of the known books; it is the pull toward the new apocryphal text still to be rediscovered or invented.

In his Norton Lectures, *Six Memos for the Next Millennium*, a work not quite complete at his death in 1985, Calvino speaks of *Invisible Cities* as "the book in which I think I managed to say most." He achieves this in the face of the most scrupulous sense of the difficulty of saying anything—as distinct, for example, from merely asserting things or announcing them, or pretending you have said them. Calvino loves and distrusts and displaces language, drives it to its limits and beyond them, devises tests and defeats for it. It would be a mistake, I think, not to take seriously his conviction that language is often a form of failure rather than success. "When you kill, you always kill the wrong man," he says in a gloss of the story of Hamlet in *The Castle of Crossed Destinies*. It's not that Hamlet is "incapable of killing": "Why, that is the only thing he succeeds in doing!" First Polonius, then Rosencrantz and Guildenstern, then Laertes, finally Claudius. Is Claudius the wrong man? Well, if he's the right man, he comes pretty late in the series. And Calvino's fiction, with its dazzled and dazzling allusions to the denser meanings of the visible world, is a monument to one of literature's most important half-truths: when you write, you always write the wrong book. Of course, you have to write pretty well for this proposition to make any interesting sense, and the other half of the truth is that the wrong book can also be just right. There are failures and failures.

II

Calvino's failure is substantial and willed, a discreet and calculated punctuation of silence. Marco Polo and Kublai Kahn, in *Invisible Cities*, converse among the fountains and magnolias of the Khan's hanging garden. At first, the Venetian is unable to speak the Khan's language, and can recount his travels in the empire only with gestures, leaps, and cries, and by exhibiting various objects he has brought back with him. He also resorts to pantomime:

> One city was depicted by the leap of a fish escaping the cormorant's beak to fall into a net; another city by a naked man running through fire unscorched; a third by a skull, its teeth green with mold, clenching a round, white pearl. The Great Khan deciphered the signs, but the connection between them and the places visited remained uncertain; he never knew whether Marco wished to enact an adventure that had befallen him on his journey, an exploit of the city's founder, the prophecy of an astrologer, a rebus or a charade to indicate a name. But, obscure or obvious as it might be, everything Marco displayed had the power of emblems, which, once seen, cannot be forgotten or confused.

Before long Marco masters the Tartar idiom (or the Emperor begins to understand Italian), and the dialogue proceeds with greater precision. But then a certain nostalgia for the emblem sets in: "You would have said communication between them was less happy than in the past."

Marco Polo and the Great Khan experience the shift from gestures to words chiefly as a loss. Words are more precise, of course, "more useful than objects or gestures in listing the most important things of every province and city," but Marco Polo finds he can't put the daily life of those places into words, and goes back to "gestures, grimaces, glances."

> So, for each city, after the fundamental information given in precise words, he followed with a mute commentary, holding up his hands, palms out, or backs, or sideways, in straight or oblique movements, spasmodic or slow. A new kind of dialogue was established: the Great Khan's white hands, heavy with rings, answered with stately movements the sinewy, agile hands of the merchant.

But then this language in turn becomes stable, conventional, closed. "The pleasure of falling back on it also diminished in both; in their conversations, most of the time, they remained silent and immobile."

We must guard against too literal a reading of this situation. The decay of dialogue is part of the beautifully elegiac and speculative movement of the whole of *Invisible Cities*, which begins with the Khan seeing his vast empire as a sumptuous, corrupt ruin and takes us deeper and deeper into his melancholy, his "sense of emptiness" and loss. We are repeatedly invited to wonder whether anything of what we read is actually happening, even within the world of the fiction. Do the Khan and Marco Polo, historical figures already thoroughly reimagined in the mind of the writer, really communicate with each other in this story, or do they dream they do? "The foreigner had learned to speak the emperor's language or the emperor to understand the language of the foreigner." This is to say they had turned to words, but not to whose words. And the supposed communication is often located more openly within the minds of the characters: "Marco Polo imagined interrupting him, or Marco Polo imagined himself interrupted"; "Marco Polo could explain or imagine explaining or to be imagined explaining or succeed finally in explaining to himself." The characters imagine themselves to be in dialogue, which is a way of saying that we have to imagine them at it, and that is the dialogue we imagine that matters. The book raises further doubts about the (fictional) reality of the speakers by having them wonder philosophically who and where they are. "Perhaps," Marco Polo says, "this garden exists only in the shadow of our lowered eyelids, and we have never stopped: you, from raising dust on the fields of battle; and I, from bargaining for sacks of pepper in distant bazaars. . . ." "Perhaps," Kublai Khan replies, "this dialogue of ours is taking place between two beggars nicknamed Kublai Khan and Marco Polo; as they sift through a rubbish heap, piling up rusted flotsam, scraps of cloth, wastepaper, while drunk on the few sips of bad wine, they see all the treasures of the East shine around them."

There are fabulous cities here, architectural dreams, haunting conclusions to scarcely imaginable journeys. Each city is a story—"Tell me another city," the Great Khan says to Marco Polo at one point. There are cities of intricate memory—"the special quality of this city for the man who arrives there on a September evening . . . is that he feels envy toward those who now believe they have once before lived an evening identical to this and who think they were happy, that time"—cities of desire, cities of signs, cities of the living and the dead. There is a city you can't arrive in, which is only the city you see as you approach; there is a city which "knows only departures"; another is all outskirts, which has no center that anyone can reach.

Certain cities have an ecological look, or the look of an ecological parody. Leonia discards so much rubbish that it piles up like mountains on all sides of the city. This rubbish would take over the globe if other cities were not doing just as Leonia does. "Perhaps the whole world, beyond Leonia's boundaries, is covered by craters of rubbish, each surrounding a metropolis in constant eruption. The boundaries between the alien, hostile cities are infected ramparts where the detritus of both support each other, overlap, mingle." The situation is dangerous: "a tin can, an old tire, an unraveled wine flask, if it rolls toward Leonia, is enough to bring with it an avalanche of unmated shoes, calendars of bygone years, withered flowers, submerging the city in its own past. . . ."

Above all there are cities within cities, implied or invisible or unknown second worlds within or alongside second worlds, dreams within dreams. The city of Valdrada, for instance, is built on the shores of a lake, and the traveler always sees the city and its exact reflection. "Nothing exists or happens in the one Valdrada that the other Valdrada does not repeat, because the city was so constructed that its every point would be reflected in its mirror. . . ." When the inhabitants of the shoreside city make love or murder each other those gestures are repeated in the lake, and "it is not so much their copulating or murdering that matters as the copulating or murdering of the images, limpid and cold in the mirror." Of course the mirror image is not exactly the same: it is a symmetrical inversion. "The two Valdradas live for each other, their eyes interlocked; but there is no love between them."

Another double city allows Marco Polo (and Calvino) a light and perfectly placed gag, a simple reversal but one we are not ready for. "Sophronia is made up of two half-cities": the fairground city, with its roller coaster, Ferris wheel, circus tent; the solid city of "stone and marble and cement," with its bank, factories, palaces, slaughterhouse, school.

One of the half-cities is permanent, the other is temporary, and when the period of its sojourn is over, they uproot it, dismantle it, and take it off, transplanting it to the vacant lots of another half-city.

And so every year the day comes when the workmen remove the marble pediments, lower the stone walls, the cement pylons, take down the Ministry, the monument, the docks, the petroleum refinery, the hospital, load them on trailers. . . .

The situation of the city of Beersheba is more complicated. Its inhabitants believe that their terrestrial city is shadowed by a celestial one where all their "most elevated virtues and sentiments" are stored, and by a subterranean one, "the receptacle of everything base and unworthy that happens to them." They are right about the two shadow cities but wrong in their identification of them: the supposed celestial city is really infernal, driven only by a "grim mania to fill the empty vessel of itself"; the supposed infernal city, a place of waste and neglect and refusal, is the real celestial city, representing the "only moments of generous abandon" known to Beersheba, "a city which only when it shits, is not miserly, calculating, greedy." Similarly, although in a different register, the city of Raissa is full of sadness, and doesn't recognize the scattered moments of happiness which are also part of its fabric, the "invisible thread that binds one living being to another, then unravels, then is stretched again between moving points as it draws new and rapid patterns so that at every second the unhappy city contains a happy city unaware of its own existence."

Andria is built according to a celestial pattern. Its denizens live, the traveler assumes, in an unchanging world, an elegant reflection of the "meticulous clockwork" of heaven. He is right about the reflection, but the inhabitants are astonished that he should think the place doesn't change. They point to the ceaseless shifts and new buildings of the city. But then what about the matching with the stars? "Our city and the sky correspond so perfectly," they answered, "that any change in Andria involves some novelty among the stars." The astronomers, after each change takes place in Andria, peer into their telescopes and report a nova's explosion, or a remote point in the firmament's change of color from orange to yellow, the expansion of a nebula, the bending of a spiral of the Milky Way. Each change implies a sequence of other changes, in Andria as among the stars: the city and the sky never remain the same. This is why the inhabitants of Andria are so confident and so prudent. "Convinced that every innovation in the city influences the sky's pattern, before taking any decision they calculate the risks and advantages for themselves and for the city and for all worlds."

In the city of Eudoxia, the mirror and secret design of the place is found in a carpet. This is at first sight surprising, since the city is full of "winding alleys, dead ends," refusals of straight lines and symmetry.

> At first sight nothing seems to resemble Eudoxia less than
> the design of that carpet. . . . But if you pause and examine it
> carefully, you become convinced that each place in the carpet
> corresponds to a place in the city and all the things contained in
> the city are included in the design, arranged according to their
> true relationship, which escapes your eye distracted by the bustle,
> the throngs, the shoving.

The stars are part of the city's sense of itself too. When an oracle was
asked about the mysterious resemblance of the carpet and the city, it said
one of those objects had "the form the gods gave the starry sky and the
orbits in which the worlds revolve," while the other was "an approximate
reflection, like every human creation." For some time the interpreters were
sure that the carpet mirrored the work of the gods and the city represented
human labor.

> But you could, similarly, come to the opposite conclusion:
> that the true map of the universe is the city of Eudoxia, just as it
> is, a stain that spreads out shapelessly, with crooked streets,
> houses that crumble one upon the other amid clouds of dust,
> fires, screams in the darkness.

No city seems to be able to live without some sort of refraction of
perfection as its opposite or model or echo. This is clearest of all in the last
two cities Marco Polo describes. Theodora banishes, destroys the whole
animal kingdom, leaving no other species than man in existence. Anyone
who wants to know about the old fauna will have to look it up in one of
Theodora's wellstocked libraries. And yet, the animals return: not the former
animals, but the wildest animals in the books, leaping from the pages in the
library, perching on the edge of the citizens' sleep. "Sphinxes, griffons,
chimera, dragons, hirocervi, harpies, hydras, unicorns, basilisks were
resuming possession of their city." Berenice is described as "the unjust city,"
but it contains a just city within it, the hope of tomorrow. However, that city
in turn will contain the seeds of its opposite, injustice stirring in the heart of
justice itself. The cities are not sequential, however.

> From my words you will have reached the conclusion that
> the real Berenice is a temporal succession of different cities,
> alternately just and unjust. But what I wanted to warn you about
> is something else: all the future Berenices are already present in
> this instant, wrapped one within the other, confined, crammed,
> inextricable.

Marco Polo's warning anticipates the wonderful last words of this book. The Khan thinks this quest for cities is finally hopeless. The perfect city will never be found, even by putting some sort of ideal city together from the pieces of all the rest. "The last landing place can only be the infernal city." Marco Polo doesn't disagree, but replaces all the implicit worries about paradise with the stronger, more practical suggestion of a resistance to hell. The inferno, he says, if there is one, is where we already live, "what is already here." There are two ways to escape the sufferings of hell, Polo suggests:

> The first is easy for many: accept the inferno and become such a part of it that you can no longer see it. The second is risky and demands constant vigilance and apprehension: seek and learn to recognize who and what, in the midst of the inferno, are not inferno, then make them endure, give them space.

But even if we are careful not to take too literally the question of language in *Invisible Cities*, we still need to attend the remarkable moment when Marco Polo rescues the Khan's empire from a desolate and terminal abstraction by "reading" his chessboard.

> Returning from his last mission, Marco Polo found the Khan awaiting him, seated at a chessboard. With a gesture he invited the Venetian to sit opposite him and describe, with the help only of the chessmen, the cities he had visited. Marco did not lose heart. The Great Khan's chessmen were huge pieces of polished ivory: arranging on the board looming rooks and sulky knights, assembling swarms of pawns, drawing straight or oblique avenues like a queen's progress, Marco recreated the perspective and the spaces of black and white cities on moonlit nights. . . . Now Kublai Khan no longer had to send Marco Polo on distant expeditions: he kept him playing endless games of chess.

The empire becomes a game; a game is an empire. But what is a game? "Each game ends in a gain or a loss," the Khan thinks, "but of what? What were the true stakes?"

> By disembodying his conquests to reduce them to the essential, Kublai had arrived at the extreme operation: the definitive conquest, of which the empire's multiform treasures were only illusory envelopes. It was reduced to a square of planed wood: nothingness. . . .

At this point, for the only time in the book, the linguistic situation is made perfectly clear: Marco Polo fluently speaks the language of the Khan. Yet it is not the fluency that amazes the Emperor, but what that fluency permits, an extraordinary combination of vision and articulation. Without the vision, there would be nothing to say; without the articulation, almost nothing of this vision could be evoked, since it is a vision of absence, of just what images cannot show. They can show the traces of absent people and things, of course, but the reading of those traces requires a syntax, a logic which goes beyond that of visual juxtaposition or sequence.

What Marco Polo sees in the chessboard, to be more precise, is not exactly an absence, but a presence filled with other, older presences, the past of the present case, what was there (here) before the chessboard became what it now is.

> "Your chessboard, sire, is inlaid with two woods: ebony and maple. The square on which your enlightened gaze is fixed was cut from the ring of a trunk that grew in a year of drought: you see how its fibers are arranged? . . . Here is a thicker pore: perhaps it was a larvum's nest; not a woodworm, because, once born it would have begun to dig, but a caterpillar that gnawed the leaves and was the cause of the tree's being chosen for chopping down . . . . This edge was scored by the wood carver with his gouge so that it would adhere to the next square, more protruding . . . ." The quantity of things that could be read in a little piece of smooth and empty wood overwhelmed Kublai; Polo was already talking about ebony forests, about rafts laden with logs that come down the rivers, of docks, of women at the windows. . . .

Calvino sees "the use of words . . . as a perpetual pursuit of things, as a perpetual adjustment to their infinite variety." You could look at the inlay and fibers and scorings of the chessboard without needing words—although you might have needed words to learn some of the things that helped you to look closely enough. But you couldn't read the board's richness without words, or make clear that your reading was a reading. It is only in words that you would be able to speak of the "trunk that grew in a year of drought," and a long dead caterpillar and a probably dead woodcarver, and the rafts and logs and docks of the past, and the imagined women at the windows of the mind.

III

In the frame story, in both frame stories, of *The Castle of Crossed Destinies*, a group of travelers is struck dumb by some terrible, unnamed experience, and each can tell his or her story only by pointing to and arranging in sequence certain cards of the tarot pack. The suggestion, it seems, is that we can abstain from the excessive and illusory clarities of verbal language only through some sort of calamity, as here, or through a shift beyond our own linguistic boundaries, like Marco Polo's travels to China. Calvino reinforces this suggestion by retaining all the noises around the travelers—"the drumming of spoons, the rattle of goblets and crockery . . . the sounds of chewing and the smacking of lips gulping wine"—so that we understand that speech is what is lost, not sound. These are people, we may say, not without language but without a language, without the langauge they think of as their own, without what we mostly think of as language. The tarot cards "conceal more things than they tell," we learn at one point, but they tell plenty, and the travelers are eager to get hold of them, to signal and recount their own adventures: "As soon as a card says more, other hands immediately try to pull it in their direction, to fit it into a different story."

The urge to tell stories survives language, finds languages of its own. The ambiguity of the images on the cards is an opportunity, not just a compensation or replacement for the speech that is lost, but a new field, a place where stories glitter and mingle as they cannot do in other modes. "Each story runs into another story," Calvino says, and "the same cards, presented in a different order, often change their meaning." The besieged city represented in the tarot of the World, for instance, is both Paris and Troy, a celestial city in yet another story, and a subterranean city in still another one.

The tarot pack, Calvino says, is "a machine for constructing stories," and he allows the look of the cards, rather than any occult meaning, to speak to him. He sees forests, for example, wherever crossed staves begin to look thick on the ground, and the King of Swords followed by the Ten of Swords produces this wonderful effect:

> Our eyes seemed suddenly blinded by the great dust cloud of battles: we heard the blare of trumpets, already the shattered spears were flying; already the clashing horses' muzzles were drenched in iridescent foam; already the swords, with the flat or the cutting edge, were striking against the flat or cutting edge of other swords. . . .

Calvino is working with two versions of the pack: the sumptuous Visconti deck, painted by Bembo, and the fairly common Marseilles deck, which can be bought in any decent occultist's shop. For the first deck, he imagines travelers staying at a castle, or perhaps an inn—the place is rather too grand for an inn, and rather too disorderly for a castle. Their stories are those of an unfaithful lover, of an unpunished grave robber, of a man who met the Devil's bride. We also hear of Faust, and of Roland as he is portrayed in Ariosto. The narrator's interpretations of the cards that are displayed are confident but frankly speculative, articulated through phrases like "our fellow guest probably wished to inform us," "this row of cards . . . surely announced," and "we could only venture some guesses"; and when he needs the story of Astolpho, the English knight in Ariosto who recovers Roland's wits for him, he seems simply to conscript a fellow guest, who "might well be that English knight." The narrator doesn't tell us his own tale, but it is there, he says, buried in the pattern the cards make on the table once several criss-crossing stories have been dealt out. More precisely, he says his story is there but he can "no longer say which it is," and a little later announces that he has "lost" his story, "confused it in the dust of the tales, become freed of it." The hint, an echo of Borges perhaps, is that everyone has a story but that those who tell many stories lose their own, not because it is buried or repressed but because it is dispersed, played out in all kinds of figurative or displaced forms. "A man," Borges writes,

> sets himself the task of sketching the world. Through the years he peoples a space with images of provinces, kingdoms, mountains, bays, ships, islands, fishes, rooms, instruments, stars, horses and persons. Shortly before dying, he discovers that this patient labyrinth of lines traces the image of his face.

For the second deck Calvino imagines another set of silent travelers, but they seem more clearly to be at an inn, as befits the less aristocratic nature of the cards themselves, and for some reason the stories deduced from these cards are much more vivid and ingenious. They include the tale of the waverer, a narrative that finds impossible choices at every turn of the card, and also the stories of Faust (again) and Parsifal, and of Hamlet, Macbeth, and Lear. At one point Calvino decides to interpret the picture card of the Pope as signifying a latinized Freud, "the great shepherd of souls and interpreter of dreams Sigismund of Vindobona," and starts to look for, and of course soon finds, the story of Oedipus in the pack, "that story which, according to the teachings of [Sigismund's] doctrine, is hidden in the warp of all stories." In the deck the writer does dig out his own tale, but it is a tale of writing, not a confession of wordly adventures or sentimental secrets. Among his cards are the Devil, because "the raw material of writing" is "a rising to the surface of hairy claws, cur-like scratching, goat's goring, repressed violences that grope in the darkness," and the Juggler, a figure "who arranges on a stand at a fair a certain number of objects and, shifting them, connecting them, interchanging them, achieves a certain number of effects." Among his models are Stendhal and the Marquis de Sade, because "in writing, what speaks is what is repressed." If we are lucky. Calvino worries a little about the portentousness of some of this—"will I not have been too pontifical?" (*troppo edificante*) he says a little later—and has his narrator deflate his own claims even as he makes them. "Writing, in short, has a subsoil which belongs to the species, or at least to civilization, or at least to certain income brackets."

In such a view, or in such an income bracket, the tarot pack is not only a machine for constructing stories, it is a labyrinth where all the world's stories can be found. But they have to be found, and finding them, it seems, does not interfere with the inexhaustible mystery of the labyrinth itself, which is organized, Calvino says, around "the chaotic heart of things, the center of the square of the cards and of the world, the point of intersection of all possible orders." Calvino experiments briefly (and brilliantly) with "reading" other pictures in the same way, famous paintings of Saint Jerome and Saint George, for example, and he says he thought of completing his "Castle of Crossed Destinies" (the Visconti pack) and "Tavern of Crossed Destinies" (the Marseilles pack) with a "Motel of Crossed Destinies," in which the mute survivors of an unnamed catastrophe would tell their tales by pointing to the various frames of the comics page of a scorched newspaper.

In the last chapter of *The Castle of Crossed Destinies* Calvino "discovers" the stories of Hamlet, Macbeth, and King Lear, described as "Three Tales of Madness and Destruction," lurking among the tarot cards already laid out, already used for other stories. He can do this, of course, only if he and we are willing to believe that almost any story can be found in the tarot deck, and we know these stories already, so the idea of reading takes an interesting turn here. The images of the cards no longer suggest to us stories we do not know and must piece together, or stories we have lived and wish to communicate to others, but stories we can, with a little ingenuity, recognize in the images set before us—stories we literally discover, or discover again.

The stories are "told" by, attributed to, members of the company in the tavern of crossed destinies, who are identified first as "a young man," "a lady" and "an old man," later as Hamlet, Lady Macbeth, and Lear. The attribution of the Macbeth story to Lady Macbeth—she is the one who thinks about the witches and their prophecies, sees Banquo's ghost; it is her life, more lucid than her husband's, that the witches make nonsense of—is a delicate shift, consistent with the focusing on madness in these narratives. The card of the Ruined Tower is Elsinore and its haunted battlements in the night; it is Dunsinane, Birnam Wood advancing upon it; it is Lear's castle, from which he has been driven, "emptied from the walls like a can of rubbish"—the card shows figures falling, a tilted crown at the top of the tower, a feather licking at the broken edifice, perhaps representing lightning, perhaps an emblematic suggestion of how lightly the agencies of destruction may seem to proceed. The card of the Moon is the night in which Hamlet's father's ghost walks; the night the witches invoke and in which they work; the blasted landscape which is all Lear has left of his possessions. The card of the Hermit is Polonius in the arras, Banquo's ghost, or perhaps even Macbeth himself, the man "who has murdered sleep" and stalks the guest rooms of his castle; and Lear on the heath, with the Fool (another card) as "his only support and mirror of his madness." The card of the Star, which depicts a set of stars and a naked woman pouring water from two pitchers, is Ophelia gone mad; Lady Macbeth seeking to wash away the stain that nothing will remove; and (in a little riff Calvino has added to the story, or found in the cards) Cordelia in exile, "drinking water from the ditches" and depending on the birds for her nourishment. The Chariot, finally, is Fortinbras come to clear up the mess in Elsinore; Malcolm arriving to assume his rightful place on the throne of Scotland; and the King of France, Cordelia's husband, crossing the channel a little too late to save the mad king and his murdered daughter.

Other cards overlap in two of the three stories—Hamlet plays the Fool and meditates on the Fool's skull; Temperance, represented by another lady with pitchers, this time pouring water from one into the other, is both Ophelia and the virtue that Lear has lost, perhaps the daughter he has lost for lack of that virtue—and some cards appear in only one story. The whole thing is a virtuoso exercise on Calvino's part, lightly done, full of mischief and amusement. Hamlet's method in his madness becomes, "If this is neurosis, there is a method in it, and in every method, neurosis." Both *Hamlet* and Lear are seen as plays about problems between the generations, the young haunted by the authority of the old, the old beset by everything the young refuse to buy. "With daughters, whatever a father does is wrong: authoritarian or permissive, parents can never expect to be thanked." The Macbeth marriage is one of equals: "They have shared the roles like a devoted couple, marriage is the encounter of two egoisms that grind each other reciprocally and from which spread the cracks in the foundations of civilized society. . . ." The suggestion of anachronism, of twentieth-century tackiness creeping up on these august old tales, mocks us gently for thinking we could tame and understand such wildnesses. We have found the stories, they are stories we know; but in what sense do we know them?

The largest suggestion here, though—and Calvino's placing of this material at the end of his book is important—is that these stories, found in this way, take us deeper into reading than we have probably been before, deeper into what reading is. Calvino's interpretations are not simply imposed on the cards—not any cards would do for any story—but they are not simply taken from the cards either. The stories are familiar already, but still need finding, and finding is itself a notion we now need to linger over a little. To discover the (very different) watery associations of Ophelia and Lady Macbeth in a particular card, as Calvino elsewhere finds the figure of the writer in the King of Clubs, who does indeed, in the Marseilles pack, seem to be holding something that looks like a ballpoint pen, is not to read these cards according to an intention ascribed to them, it is to make associations, whether theatrical and Shakespearean or technical and twentieth century. The associations may operate as a joke, like the ballpoint pen, or as an extension of a metaphorical universe, like the water in the card of the Star.

There is a sense here of the curious, punning crossover between one fiction and another, or between fiction and fact, which we meet when characters from novels by Cortazar and Fuentes show up in a novel by Garcia Marquez, or when we read about the Gents' Outfitters shop in Dublin, both Joyce's and history's, which is called Henry and James. The names are common enough in the second case, there is no mystery here; but for a moment the city seems mischievously to refer to a famous writer, to make a literary joke, and Joyce didn't miss it; recorded it for us, precisely, since the shop has gone and the text remains. There is a more elaborate instance of such interplay between given and taken associations in Pynchon's *Gravity's Rainbow*. The German pronunciation of the letter V is *fau* (rhymes with how), so that the names of V-1 and V-2 rockets sound like the word for a peacock, a *Pfau*, whose tail when spread has the color of the rainbow, and the shape of the rainbow and of the trajectory of those rockets as they fly from north Germany to England: gravity's rainbow. The deliberate construction of such a network of associations, either by the novelist or by the critic, would be an absurd piece of pedantry. As it is, it would be pretty pedantic to brood on it much. But there surely is an eerie little shock here, as if we had stumbled on an order we had not suspected and which is not ours. The German language, or a pun which is lurking in this language and not in others, seems to connect the rocket with the peacock and to bring natural and technical shapes and colors together in the wake of this connection. Dublin similarly, not Joyce, made the joke Joyce found.

Yet of course Joyce, or someone, had to find it. Perhaps both writing and reading are larger affairs than our narrow notions of communication allow; and certainly reading understood as finding pieces of a world, as distinct from imagining whole worlds, assembled, disassembled, reassembled, has a peculiar richness of its own. We can't dispense with the imagination, of course—there is no reading without it, and not much life of any kind—but we shouldn't allow it all the honors, exclusively. The world as it is has surprises for us too; to impose, as Stevens said, is not to discover.

And then it's important that single cards can be read in so many different ways. Here I interpret Calvino as suggesting—I interpret his text as allowing us to think—that the images of the tarot pack may not only remind us of everything articulated language flattens and misses, and not only invite us to pick up the dialogue between image and speech so beautifully dramatized in Marco Polo's reading of the Great Khan's cheesboard, but they may also picture for us language itself in its most ordinary sense: what words are like. They are not just the pale and harassed servants we push around when we want to get things, ask for directions, food, love. Words, even the smallest, most insignificant-seeming, most abused of them, are pictures of life; they have histories and complications and multiple uses. When you say tower you might mean a card in the tarot pack, or Paris, or Blackpool, or London; just as the card may mean Elsinore or Dunsinane or the castle Lear has lost. Words are cards; you can play them in functional sentences; you can tell fortunes in them and tell stories; you can read stories in them, above all, in this context, the stories that hide in or accompany the stories ostensibly being told. "In writing, what speaks is what is repressed." We don't have to hold Calvino to this remark as to declaration of fatih. But "writing" here might be taken as a metaphor borrowed from Derrida. Writing, whether materially set down, or spoken aloud, or mentally pursued, is looking at words to see the pictures in them, to glimpse the other, possible stories they offer, as well as the stories they have been conscripted to tell.

The question of language reminds us of the irony which is lurking everywhere in *The Castle of Crossed Destinies:* we are not reading the stories in the tarot cards, we are not even in the room with the narrator who is reading them. The narrator has translated the mute speech of the cards into Italian, and Calvino has reported his activities in print—and we have read the whole thing in English. The silence of the cards is repeated in the silence of the page, and (perhaps) in the silence of the room in which we read. But the pictorial amibiguities of the cards, their worlds of possibility, have been turned into consecutive, grammatical language. The celebration of emblems must leave the realm of emblems behind, cannot do without the supplementary clues and markings of language in its most familiar sense. There is a dialogue, let's say, between the riches of imagery and the directedness of speech or writing, and it is the dialogue that matters rather than the riches or the directedness on their own. Or we need images as a reminder of everything language simplifies or misses, and we may believe that a language which remembered this would be different and renewed.

IV

The central character of Calvino's *Mr. Palomar* would like to learn a modest lesson or two from the unexplained world. But of course, as we have seen, the simplest things and creatures shimmer with complication when we look at them closely. What was richness and restoration of the world for Marco Polo will seem like invasive human history, or depredation by selfconsciousness, if we are trying to get back to nature. This is how we meet Mr. Palomar, on the first page of the book:

> The sea is barely wrinkled, and little waves strike the sandy shore. Mr. Palomar is standing on the shore, looking at a wave. Not that he is lost in contemplation of the waves. He is not lost, because he is quite aware of what he is doing: he wants to look at a wave and he is looking at it. He is not contemplating, because for contemplation you need the right temperament, the right mood, and the right combination of exterior circumstances . . . Finally it is not "the waves" that he means to look at, but just one individual wave. . . .

Mr. Palomar "vacillates at length," Calvino says, and indeed the character's life on the page consists of lengthy, strenuous vacillation. But then Calvino's patience with Mr. Palomar's amiable pedantry—or rather Calvino's ironic invention of Palomar and pedantry and the precise and relaxed prose which pursues them—produces wonderful effects. The individual wave is lost, but an indirect, unexpectedly beautiful description of the sea takes its place:

> And so the wave continues to grow and gain strength until the clash with contrary waves gradually dulls it and makes it disappear, or else twists it until it is confused in one of the many dynasties of oblique waves slammed, with them, against the shore.

Mr. Palomar has a swim, thinks about naked bosoms on beaches—is it a sign of prejudice to avert your eyes? He listens to a pair of blackbirds and wonders whether their signals are very different from those he exchanges with his wife. "The equal whistle of man and blackbird now seems to him a bridge thrown over the abyss. . . ." An albino gorilla, lost in his biological loneliness, hugs a rubber tire as if he knew what a symbol was. This, Mr. Palomar thinks, is how we seek to escape from "the dismay of living: investing oneself in things, recognizing oneself in signs."

The albino gorilla is a type nature has produced but not preferred, "sole exemplar in the world of a form not chosen, not loved"; even his mate and his offspring are black like other gorillas. "Mr. Palomar feels he understands the gorilla perfectly," Calvino tells us, inviting us to smile at his hero's presumption; but it is likely that Mr. Palomar does understand, if not the gorilla, then something of the gorilla's condition as extravagant remnant of a road not taken: a possibility actualized once and only once. It is this strange dialogue with possibility which draws Mr. Palomar to the reptile house in the Jardin des Plantes in Paris. The iguana, for instance, looks like "a sample-case of forms available in the animal kingdom and perhaps also in other kingdoms: too much stuff for one animal to bear." If the gorilla is (almost) no one, the iguana is everyone. The whole reptile house suggests to Mr. Palomar "a squandering of forms without style and without plan, where all is possible." But then only certain forms—"perhaps actually the most incredible"— become finally fixed and identifiable in natural history, classifiable in the cases of a zoo. They are that history, "the order of the world," and it may be that what Mr. Palomar likes is the thought of "the world as it was before man, or after"; the chance, as he thinks, to be someone "who peers out beyond the human." But of course every sample in the zoo is torn from whatever life it lived in nature, and preserved in an artificial climate. Far from being the order of the world before or after man, this is the very order of the human, the place where the world is our representation and our hypothesis. It's at this point that the smell of the reptile house becomes unbearable to Mr. Palomar, and he gives up wondering about the appeal of the iguanas. They are replaced (in his immediate experience, the bestiary of his mind) by a group of brilliantly described, inscrutable crocodiles.

> Is theirs a boundless patience, or a desperation without end? What are they waiting for, or what have they given up waiting for? In what time are they immersed? In that of the species, removed from the course of the hours that race from the birth to the death of the individual? Or in the time of geological eras that shifts continents and solidifies the crust of emerged lands? Or in the slow cooling of the rays of the sun? The thought of a time outside our experience is intolerable. Mr. Palomar hurries to leave the snake house. . . .

Mr. Palomar takes himself to the edge of the human, finds there more humanity than he wants, and then encounters a darker, more frightening sense of the world without us. The human is in one sense inescapable, in another it is what we cannot bear the thought of escaping from: the first because of the second, perhaps. Knowledge for Calvino means seeing what we have done to the world, how littered it is with our decisions and interpretations; but it also means giving up our grasp of the world, fostering a loyalty to everything which persists beyond or beneath or apart from our interpretations. This intractable stuff wouldn't necessarily be blank or uninterpreted, purely natural—it's actually quite hard to see what the notion would mean, since the concept of nature is itself the product of ancient and proliferating interpretations. But it would elude our interpretations; there are whole universes, large and small, to remind us of the fullness rather than the emptiness of silence.

Perhaps the deepest and funniest moment in *Mr. Palomar* occurs in the account of our hero's visit to a prehispanic ruin at Tula, in Mexico. His Mexican friend is "an impassioned and eloquent expert," full of stories about Quetzalcoatl, the god-king who takes the form of a plumed serpent, and about extravagant coyotes and jaguars. "Mr. Palomar's friend pauses at each stone, transforms it into a cosmic tale, an allegory, a moral reflection." At the same time a group of schoolboys is being taken round the ruins. At each stone, or pyramid, or statue, their teacher provides copious factual details—date, civilization, building material—and adds each time, "We don't know what it means." Mr. Palomar "is fascinated by his friend's wealth of mythological references: the play of interpretation, allegorical readings, have always seemed to him a supreme exercise of the mind." But there is a humility of the mind, too, and Mr. Palomar is also drawn to what he takes to be the teacher's position, a "refusal to comprehend more than what the stones show us," which is "perhaps the only way to evince respect for their secret."

The teacher leads the boys to the beautiful Wall of the Serpents. "This is the wall of the serpents. Each serpent has a skull in its mouth. We don't know what they mean." Mr. Palomar's friend can stand it no longer, and cries, "Yes, we do! It's the continuity of life and death; the serpents are life, the skulls are death. Life is life because it bears death with it, and death is death because there is no life without death. . . ."

The boys listen, astonished. Mr. Palomar thinks his friend's interpretation is still in need of an interpretation ("What did death, life, continuity, passage mean for the ancient Toltecs?"), but knows that "not to interpret is impossible, as refraining from thinking is impossible." Impossible for us, that is. Once the school group is round the corner, the teacher says, "*No es verdad*, it is not true, what the señor said. We don't know what they mean."

We don't know; we do know; we can't bear not to know; all knowledge is frayed with ignorance, tilted over absences or further questions. "I am accustomed to consider literature a search for knowledge," Calvino says in one of his lectures, and among many other pleasures, *Six Memos for the Next Millennium* offers a beautifully paced account of Calvino's reading, a record of cherished books and images, which amounts to a discreet fragment of autobiography. Leopardi is a major presence, appears again and again; so does Lucretius. Paul Valery is Calvino's modern master, creator of Monsieur Teste, a "great intellectual personage of this century." Borges is said to have achieved Valery's aesthetic ideal, while his *Ficciones* contains "the last great invention of a new literary genre in our time." The "last real 'event' in the history of the novel so far," though, is Perec's *Life: a User's Manual.* Calvino also speaks warmly of Balzac, Flaubert, de Quincey, James, Proust, Kafka, Musil, Gadda, the comics he devoured before he was even able to read, the famous paintings he chooses to interpret as frozen stories, the cinema, another fund of images which "became an absolute obsession."

What's striking here is the extravagant appropriateness of this reading and viewing for a writer like Calvino. If Borges had invented Calvino, he would also have invented this intellectual genealogy. This is not to say Calvino is himself predictable or the victim of a modern fashion. It is to say that he has put his reading and looking to serious effect. The genealogy becomes less than a canon and more than a private journey. It is a recognizable track through modernity, a picture of some of the century's significant ghosts, the ones that haunt contemporary writing; and it allows us to wonder what writing will be like, what it will miss, when it tries to avoid or ignore a sizable proportion of the names I have just mentioned, or forgets the comics and the paintings and the movies.

Chronology

1923   Italo Calvino is born in Santiago de Las Vegas, Cuba, on October 15 to Mano Calvino and Eva Mameli Calvino, both botanists. The family immediately returns to Italy, settling in the Riviera town of San Remo. Calvino grows up in the free-thinking, scientific atmosphere surrounding the University of Turin where his father teaches. After secondary schooling, he enrolls at the university in the Faculty of Science.

1943   Disregarding official orders to enlist in the Italian army, Calvino joins the resistance and spends two years as a partisan in the Maritime Alps, fighting German and Italian fascists.

1945   Now a committed member of the Communist Party, Calvino returns to Turin to write for left-wing journals, including *L'Unità*. He gives up his scientific studies and enrolls in the Faculty of Letters. In Turin he forms close friendships with writers Elio Vittorini, Cesare Pavese, Natalia Ginsberg, and Carlo Levi. He publishes many short stories and becomes known also for a brand of militant journalism which he continues to practice through the mid-sixties.

1947   Calvino graduates with a thesis on Joseph Conrad and takes an editorial position with Giulio Einaudi, a publishing company that had recently been organized by Pavese and Ginsberg. Einaudi publishes Calvino's first novel, *Il sentiero dei nidi di ragno* (*The Path to the Nest of Spiders*), based on his experiences during the war. All of his later books are published by Einaudi.

1949   A volume of Calvino's short stories, *Ultimo viene il corvo* (*Last Comes the Crow*), is published.

1950   Cesare Pavese commits suicide. Calvino is deeply affected by the loss of his friend and senses his own socialist commitment diminishing.

1952   *Il visconte dimezzato* (*The Cloven Viscount*) is published. "La formica argentina" ("The Argentine Ant") appears in *Botteghe oscure*.

1954   *L'Entrata in guerra* (*Entry into War*) published.

1955   Calvino writes the preface for *Fiabe africane*, a volume of African folktales, published by Einaudi.

1956   *Fiabe italiane* (*Italian Folktales*) published.

1957   Calvino resigns from the Communist Party. *La speculazione edilizia* (*A Plunge into Real Estate*) and *Il Barone rampante* (*The Baron in the Trees*) published.

1958   *La nuvola di smog e la formica argentina* ("*Smog*" and "*The Argentine Ant*") published.

1959   Calvino joins Vittorini in founding *Il Menabò*, a journal to which he contributes until Vittorini's death in 1966. On his first visit to the United States he meets Kenneth Rexroth, Lionel Trilling, and other well-known writers. *Il cavaliere inesistente* (*The Nonexistent Knight*) and the short story collection *I Racconti* are published.

1960   *Il cavaliere inesistente*, *Il visconte dimezzata* and *Il barone rampante* are reissued as the trilogy *I nostri antenati* (*Our Ancestors*). In a new preface to this edition Calvino defends his departure from realism.

1963   *Marcovaldo, ovvero le stagioni in città* (*Marcovaldo, or the Seasons in the City*) and *La giornata d'uno scrutatore* (*The Watcher*) are published.

1964   Calvino moves to Paris where he becomes acquainted with such eminent French intellectuals as Claude Lévi-Strauss, Michel Foucault, and Roland Barthes. He marries Chichita Singer, an Argentinean translator for UNESCO.

1965   *Le cosmicomiche* (*Cosmicomics*) is published.

1966   Calvino's correspondence with Pavese from 1924 to 1950 is published. Vittorini dies.

1967   *Ti con zero* (*t zero*) is published.

1968   Calvino's correspondence with Vittorini is published.

1969   *Tarocchi* (*Tarot*) is published.

1970   *Gli amori difficili*, a collection of wartime and postwar stories reprinted from *Ultimo viene il corvo* and *I racconti*, is published.

1972   Calvino is awarded Premio Feltrinelli per la narrative, the most prestigious Italian literary prize. *Le città invisibili* (*Invisible Cities*) is published.

1973   *Il castello dei destini incrociati* (*The Castle of Crossed Destinies*) is published.

1979   *Se una notte d'inverno un viaggiatore* (*If On a Winter's Night a Traveler*) is published.

1980   Calvino moves to Rome with his wife and their daughter Giovanna. *Una pietra sopra: discorsi di letteratura e societá* (*The Uses of Literature*) is published.

1981   *If On a Winter's Night a Traveler,* William Weaver's translation of *Se una notte d'inverno un viaggiatore*, is published.

1982   William Weaver translates Calvino's text for the Pace Gallery
         exhibition *Saul Steinberg: Still Life and Architecture*, April
         3–May 1.

1983   *Palomar* (*Mr. Palomar*) published.

1984   Calvino accepts the Charles Eliot Norton lectureship at Harvard
         University for 1985.

1985   On September 5 Italo Calvino suffers a severe stroke. He dies in
         Siena on September 19.

Contributors

HAROLD BLOOM is Sterling Professor of the Humanities at Yale University and Henry W. and Albert A. Berg Professor of English at the New York University Graduate School. He is the author of over 20 books, including *Shelley's Mythmaking* (1959), *The Visionary Company* (1961), *Blake's Apocalypse* (1963), *Yeats* (1970), *A Map of Misreading* (1975), *Kabbalah and Criticism* (1975), *Agon: Toward a Theory of Revisionism* (1982), *The American Religion* (1992), *The Western Canon* (1994), and *Omens of Millennium: The Gnosis of Angels, Dreams, and Resurrection* (1996). *The Anxiety of Influence* (1973) sets forth Professor Bloom's provocative theory of the literary relationships between the great writers and their predecessors. His most recent books include *Shakespeare: The Invention of the Human*, a 1998 National Book Award finalist, and *How to Read and Why*, which was published in 2000. In 1999, Professor Bloom received the prestigious American Academy of Arts and Letters Gold Medal for Criticism.

GORE VIDAL is a novelist, playwright, and critic. Among his novels are *Burr* (1973), *Lincoln* (1984), *Empire* (1987), *Hollywood: A Novel of America* (1990), and *Live from Golgotha* (1992). His 1995 memoir *Palimpsest* contains reminiscences of such diverse figures as Tennessee Williams, John F. Kennedy, and Eleanor Roosevelt.

ANGELA M. JEANNET is Professor of Italian and French at Franklin and Marshall College. She has written many articles on Italian literature. Her works include two books published in 2000, *Natalia Ginzburg: A Voice of the*

Twentieth Century and *Under the Radiant Sun and the Crescent Moon: Italo Calvino's Storytelling*.

TERESA DE LAURETIS is Professor of Italian and French and Senior Fellow of the Center for Twentieth Century Studies at the University of Wisconsin. She has published extensively on literary theory, semiotics, and film. Her books include *Alice Doesn't: Feminism, Semiotics, Cinema* (1984) and *Technologies of Gender: Essays on Theory, Film, and Fiction* (1989).

OLGA RAGUSA is Da Ponte Professor of Italian at Columbia University. Her books include *Pirandello: An Approach to His Theatre* (1980) and *Mallarmé in Italy: A Study of Literary Influence and Critical Response* (1983).

LINDA C. BADLEY is Professor of English at Middle Tennessee State University. She is the author of *Film, Horror and the Body Fantastic* (1995) and *Writing Horror and the Body* (1996).

SEAMUS HEANEY, an Irish poet and essayist, won the Nobel Prize for literature in 1995. His poetic works include *Death of a Naturalist* (1966), *Field Work* (1979), *Station Island* (1985), *Seeing Things* (1991), and *The Spirit Level* (1996). He has also translated *Sweeney Astray* (1983), a medieval Irish poem, and Sophocles's *Philoctetes* (published in 1991 as *The Cure at Troy*). His translation of *Beowulf* (2000) was a *New York Times* bestseller.

JOHN DOLIS is the author of *The Style of Hawthorne's Gaze: Regarding Subjectivity* (1993).

MICHAEL WOOD is Professor of English and Comparative Literature at Princeton. His books include *The Magician's Doubt's: Nabokov and the Risks of Fiction* (1994) and *Children of Silence: On Contemporary Fiction* (1998). He is a regular contributor to the *New York Review of Books* and the *London Review of Books*.

Bibliography

Adler, Sarah Maria. *Calvino: The Writer as Fablemaker.* Baltimore: José Porrua Turnazas, 1979.

Ahern, John. "Out of Montale's Cavern: A Reading of Calvino's *Gli amori difficili.*" *Modern Language Studies* 12 (1982): 3–19.

Andrews, Richard. "Italo Calvino." In *Writers and Society in Contemporary Italy*, edited by Michael Caesar and Peter Hainsworth. Warwickshire, England: Berg Publishers, 1984.

Biasin, Gian-Paolo. "4/3IIr³ (Scientific vs. Literary Space)." *Versus* 19/20 (1978): 173–88.

Burgess, Anthony. Review of *Italian Folktales*, by Italo Calvino. *Times Literary Supplement* (9 January 1981): 29.

Calvino, Italo. *The Uses of Literature.* Translated by Patrick Creagh. New York: Harcourt Brace Jovanovich, 1986.

Cannon, JoAnn. *Italo Calvino: Writer and Critic.* Ravenna, Italy: Longo Editore, 1981.

———. "The Image of the City in the Novels of Italo Calvino." *Modern Fiction Studies* 24 (1978): 83–90.

———. "Literature as Combinatory Game: Italo Calvino's *The Castle of Crossed Destinies.*" *Criticism* 21 (1979): 83–91.

———. "Literary Signification: An Analysis of Calvino's Trilogy." *Symposium* 34 (1980): 3–12.

Davies, Russell. "The Writer Versus the Reader." *Times Literary Supplement* (10 July 1981): 773–74.

de Lauretis, Teresa. "Narrative Discourse in Calvino: Praxis or Poetis?" *PMLA* 90 (1975): 414–25.

De Mara, Nicholas A. "Pathway to Calvino: Fantasy and Realty in *The Path to the Nest of Spiders.*" *Italian Quarterly* 14 (1971): 25–49.

Enright, D. J. "Effrontery and Charm." *New York Review of Books* 11 (1968): 23.

Everman, W. D. "*The Castle of Crossed Destinies.*" *New Orleans Review* 13 (1980): 22.

Flower, Dean. Review of *Marcovaldo*, by Italo Calvino. *The Hudson Review* 37 (1984): 308–9.

Gabriele, Tommasina. *Italo Calvino: Eros and Language.* Cranbury, N.J.: Fairleigh Dickinson University Press, 1994.

Gardner, John. "'The Pilgrims' Hair Turned White." *New York Times Book Review* (10 April 1977): 1, 5.

Gatt-Rutter, John. "Calvino Ludens: Literary Play and Its Political Implications." *Journal of European Studies* 5 (1975): 319–40.

Goldberg, H. "*Italian Folktales.*" *Romance Philology* 38 (1984): 41.

Haviaras, Stratis. "Advertisement (Or, Sr. Calvino's Shaving Brush)." *Ploughshares* 11 (1986): 11–13.

Heiney, Donald. "Calvino and Borges: Some Implications of Fantasy." *Mundus Artium* 2 (1968): 66–76.

Heiney, Donald, and Eric Rabkin. *Form in Fiction.* New York: St. Martin's Press, 1976.

Hume, Kathryn. "Italo Calvino's Cosmic Comedy: Mythography for the Scientific Age." *Papers on Language and Literature* 20 (1984): 80–95.

James, Carol P. "Seriality and Narrativity in Calvino's *Le città invisibili.*" *Modern Language Notes* 97 (1982): 144–61.

Janome, Claudia J. "Plato's Fourth Bed: Italo Calvino." *New Orleans Review* 9 (1982): 37–40.

Lasdun, James. Review of *Marcovaldo*, by Italo Calvino. *Encounter* 62 (1984): 69.

Le Guin, Ursula. Review of *Italian Folktales*, by Italo Calvino. *The New Republic* 183 (1980): 33.

Lucente, G. "Signs and Science in Italo Calvino's *Cosmicomiche*: Fantascienza as Satire." *Forum Italicum* 17 (1983): 29–40.

McCarthy, Mar. "Acts of Love." *The New York Review of Books* 28 (1981): 3.

McCaffery, Larry. "Form, Formula and Fantasy: Generative Structures in Contemporary Fiction." In *Bridges to Fantasy*, edited by George E. Slusser, Eric S. Rabkin, and Robert Scholes. Carbondale: Southern Illinois University Press, 1982.

McLaughlin, Martin. "Life and Literature in Calvino's Early Works." *Association of Teachers of Italian Journal* 35 (1982): 49–59.

———. "Continuity and Innovation in Calvino's *Palomar.*" *Bulletin for the Society of Italian Studies* 17 (1984): 43–9.

Maclean, Marie. "Metamorphoses of the Signifier in 'Unnatural' Languages." *Science Fiction Studies* 11 (1984): 166–73.

MacShane, Frank. "A Novel Within a Novel." *The New Republic* 184 (1981): 34.

———. "The Fantasy World of Italo Calvino." *New York Times Magazine*, 10 July 1983.

Markey, Constance. "The Hero's Quest in Calvino." *Quaderni d'Italianistica* 4 (1983): 154–66.

———. *Italo Calvino: A Journey Toward Postmodernism.* Gainesville: University Press of Florida, 1999.

Olken, I. T. *With Pleated Eye and Garnet Wing: Symmetries of Italo Calvino.* Ann Arbor: University of Michigan Press, 1984.

Ragusa, Olga. "*Palomar.*" *World Literature Today* 59 (1985): 70.

Re, Lucia. *Calvino and the Age of Neorealism: Fables of Estrangement.* Stanford, Calif.: Stanford University Press, 1990.

Ricci, Franco. "The Readers in Italo Calvino's Latest Fabula." *Forum Italicum* 16 (1982): 82–102.

———. "*Palomar* by Italo Calvino: The (un)Covering of (un)Equivocal (un)Truth." *Quaderni d'Italianistica* 5 (1984): 236–46.

———. "Silence and Loss of Self in Italo Calvino's *Gli amori difficili.*" *Italianist* 4 (1984): 54–72.

Schneider, Marilyn. "Calvino at a Crossroads: *Il castello dei destini incrociati.*" *PMLA* 95 (1980): 73–90.

———. "Calvino's Erotic Metaphor and the Hermaphroditic Solution." *Stanford Italian Review* 2 (1981): 93–118.

Sontag, Susan. "Calvino." *Vogue* 171 (1981): 279–80.

Sutcliff, Thomas. Review of *The Baron in the Trees*, by Italo Calvino. *Times Literary Supplement* (2 September 1983): 921.

Thomson, Ian. "Life in the Trees." *Literary Review 28* (1985): 181.

Towers, Robert. Review of *Difficult Loves*, by Italo Calvino. *The New York Review of Books* 31 (1984): 33.

Updike, John. "Writers and Readers." *The New Yorker* (3 August 1981): 90–91.

Varnai, Ugo. *Review of Difficult Loves*, by Italo Calvino. *Times Literary Supplement* (29 June 1984): 716.

Vidal, Gore. "*If On a Winter's Night a Traveler*." *The New York Review of Books* 28 (1981): 3.

Valsopolos, Anca. "Love and Two Discourses in *Le cosmichomiche*." *Stanford Italian Review* 4 (1984): 123–35.

Weiss, Beno. *Understanding Italo Calvino*. Columbia: University of South Carolina Press, 1993.

Woodhouse, J. R. *Italo Calvino: A Reappraisal and Reappreciation of the Trilogy*. Hull: University of Hull, 1968.

———. "Italo Calvino: The Rediscovery of a Genre." *Italian Quarterly* 12 (1968): 45–60.

———. "Fantasy, Alienation and the Racconti of Italo Calvino." *Forum for Modern Language Studies* 6 (1970): 399–412.

———. "Rampant Nonconformity: An Orthodox Guide to Italo Calvino." *Association of Teachers of Italian Journal* 30 (1980): 23–29.

Zago, Ester. "The Romantic Baron of Italo Calvino." *Proceedings on the Pacific Northwest Conference on Foreign Languages* 28 (1977): 78–80.

Acknowledgments

"Fabulous Calvino" by Gore Vidal from *The New York Review of Books* 21, no. 9 (30 May 1974). © 1974 by *The New York Review of Books*. Reprinted by permission.

"Italo Calvino's Invisible City" by Angela M. Jeannet from *Perspectives on Contemporary Literature* 3, no. 1 (1977). © 1977 by *Perspectives on Contemporary Literature*. Reprinted by permission.

"Semiotic Models, *Invisible Cities*" by Teresa Lauretis from *Yale Italian Studies* (Winter 1978). © 1978 by *Yale Italian Studies*. Reprinted by permission.

"Italo Calvino: The Repeated Conquest of Contemporaneity" by Olga Ragusa from *World Literature Today* 57, no. 2 (Spring 1983). © 1983 by *World Literature Today*. Reprinted by permission.

"Calvino *engagé:* Reading as Resistance in *If On a Winter's Night a Traveler*" by Linda C. Badley from *Perspectives in Contemporary Literature* (1984). © 1984 by *Perspectives in Contemporary Literature*. Reprinted by permission.

"The Sensual Philosopher: *Mr. Palomar*" by Seamus Heaney from *The New York Times* (29 September 1985). © 1985 by the New York Times Company. Reprinted by permission.

"Calvino's *Cosmicomics:* Original Si(g)n" by John Dolis from *Extrapolation* 39, no. 1 (Spring 1998). © 1998 by the Kent State University Press. Reprinted by permission.

"Hidden in the Distance: Reading Calvino Reading" by Michael Wood from *The Kenyon Review* 20, no. 2 (Spring 1998). © 1998 by Kenyon College. Reprinted by permission.

Index